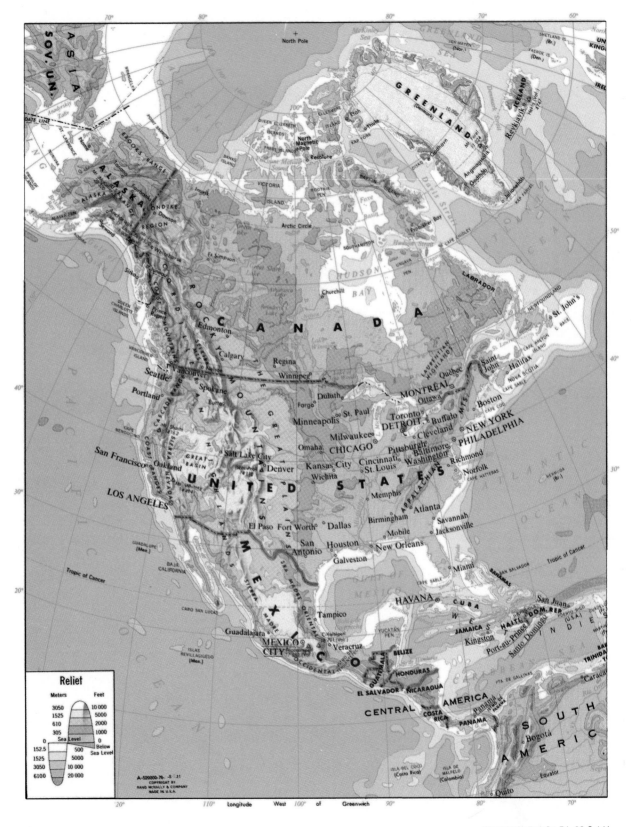

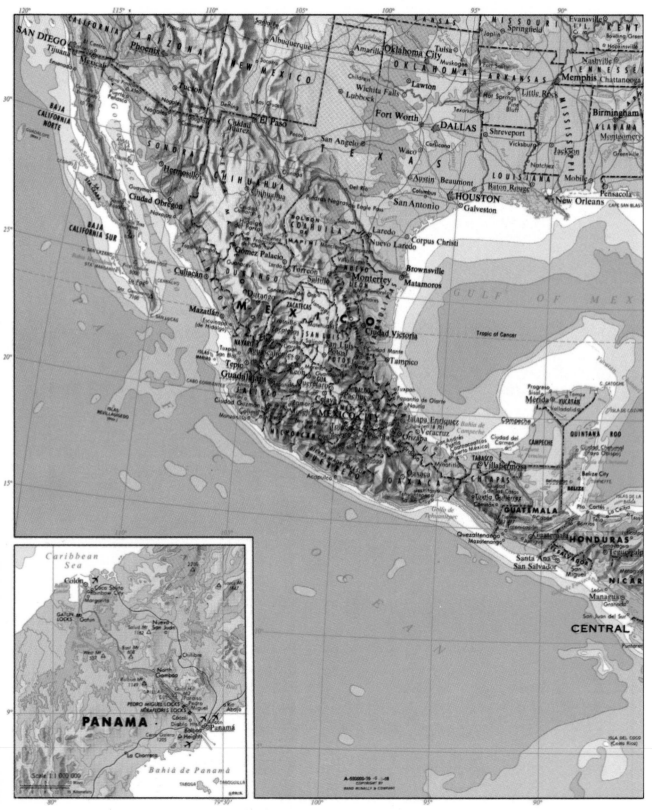

Enchantment of the World

MEXICO

by R. Conrad Stein

Consultants: John H. Coatsworth, Professor of Latin American History, The University of Chicago

Robert Somerlott, Director, Centro Internacional; Professor of Mexican Studies; former Chairman of Humanities, Instituto Allende, Incorporado con la Universidad de Guanajuato

Consultant for Social Studies: Donald W. Nylin, Ph.D., Assistant Superintendent for Instruction, Aurora West Public Schools, Aurora, Illinois

Consultant for Reading: Robert L. Hillerich, Ph.D., Bowling Green State University, Bowling Green, Ohio

 CHILDRENS PRESS, CHICAGO

Tarascan Indians use butterfly nets to catch fish in Lake Pátzcuaro.

Library of Congress Cataloging in Publication Data

Stein, R. Conrad.
  Mexico.

  (Enchantment of the world)
  Includes index.
  Summary: An introduction to the geography, history,
economy, culture, government, and people of the very
varied country of Mexico.
    1. Mexico—Juvenile literature. [1. Mexico] I. Title.
II. Series.
F1208.5.S73 1984   972   83-20898
ISBN 0-516-02772-7

Picture Acknowledgments

Hillstrom Stock Photos: ©Terry B. Whelan: Cover;
©Norma Morrison: Pages 5, 8 (right), 17 (right), 53 (right),
66 (right), 79 (left), 87 (right), 98 (right);
©D.J. Variakojis: Pages 6 (top), 25, 26, 31, 80 (right), 87;
©Milton and Joan Mann: Pages 14 (left), 18, 69, 74, 75, 78,
79 (right), 89 (left), 101 (left), 105, 106, 121;
©Connie McCollum: Pages 46, 53 (left), 83 (left);
©Carol Nero: Page 83 (right);
©Raymond F. Hillstrom: Page 84
Colour Library International: Pages 4, 8 (left), 11
(bottom), 12, 17 (left), 24, 40, 76, 88 (left)
Charmayne McGee: Pages 6 (bottom), 14 (right), 29, 30,
32, 44 (left), 50, 68, 70, 71, 73, 80 (left), 88 (right), 90, 92, 93,
97 (right), 101 (right), 104, 107, 110, 123
Eugenia Fawcett: Pages 11 (top), 43, 66 (left), 96, 97 (left),
98 (left), 120
Root Resources: ©Byron Crader: Pages 20, 22, 44 (right),
65; ©Mary Root: Page 51
© Irene E. Hubbell: Page 58
Metropolitan Museum of Art: The Michael C. Rockefeller
Memorial Collection of Primitive Art, Bequest of Nelson
A. Rockefeller, 1979: Pages 21, 23 (right)
Historical Pictures Service, Chicago: Pages 23 (left), 37,
57, 62
Chandler Forman: Pages 48, 89 (right), 103
Cover: Taxco

Tehuantepec women shopping in the Oaxaca market

TABLE OF CONTENTS

Pastel-colored houses and brilliant flowers bursting from pots brighten the villages and cities of Mexico.

Chapter 1

THE LAND AND PEOPLE
OF MEXICO

The first-time visitor to Mexico is dazzled by colors. Even in smog-covered Mexico City, brilliant flowers burst out of park lawns and explode from pots on windowsills. Their sharp colors seem to slash through the hazy, polluted air. In otherwise drab rural villages, a bright sun bathes houses that are often painted salmon red, orange, or powder blue.

Mexicans love the contrasts different colors produce. In fact, this fascinating country could be called a land of contrasts.

THE CONTRASTS OF MEXICO

Startling contrasts can be seen in Mexico City. In the center of the city stands a glittering hospital complex called Centro Médico. Its glass and steel buildings house the most modern medical equipment. But just a ten-minute walk from the hospital is a tumbledown shack where sick people consult a woman called a *curandera* (curer). She rolls an egg over a patient's body, then breaks the egg into a dish. By studying the form the yolk takes,

In this land of contrasts, a young girl cares for her baby sister in a neighborhood market not far from the sprawling modern metropolitan area of Mexico City.

she determines what disease is present. Perhaps she will prescribe a tea made of dried roots or leaves. She might advise the patient to pray to a certain saint.

Why would anyone go to a curandera when there is a modern clinic at the Centro Médico? Money is not the answer. Service at the Centro Médico is free for the poor, while the curandera charges a fee. Neither is backwardness the answer. Many people who visit the curandera respect modern medicine. Perhaps they have already seen a doctor. They want a second opinion from a mystical woman who treats sickness by more ancient means. A curandera working in the shadow of a modern hospital is just one of the many contrasts found in Mexico.

The streets of Mexico City present a flood of contrasts. Faces are light tan, pale white, pure black, or leathery brown. There are also great contrasts between rich and poor. Some families ride in luxurious cars. Their clothes come from shops in New York or

Paris. But walking the streets are families dressed in rags. Boys and girls only three or four years old stretch their arms out, palms up, begging for pennies. There are also contrasts in the Mexican character. A visitor asking street directions will be surprised at how friendly and helpful the Mexican people can be. But when the same visitor tries to squeeze into a crowded bus, the friendly Mexicans might suddenly turn into raging football players willing to crush anyone in their way.

Contrasts. Mexico is alive with them. A foreigner can live in the country for years, speak the Spanish language, and adopt the native customs. Still, the day will come when Mexico totally surprises that foreigner.

THE LAND OF MEXICO

Some 450 years ago, a Spanish traveler returned home after a trip to Mexico. The king of Spain summoned the traveler to his court.

"Tell me," asked the king, "what is this new land like?"

"Well, Sire," said the traveler, "Mexico is sort of. . . no, it is kind of—" The traveler curled and uncurled his fingers as if he were kneading a loaf of bread.

"Speak up!" commanded the king. "I want to know what the new land looks like."

"It's like. . . it's like—"

Finally the traveler spotted a piece of paper on the king's desk. He grabbed it and crushed it in his fist. Then he flattened the paper on the desk and let it rise so the wrinkles popped out.

"There, your majesty," he said. "That is what Mexico looks like."

The early Spaniards had never seen a land as mountainous as Mexico. The traveler described the country the best way he knew how.

Two jagged mountain ranges sweep the length of Mexico along its seacoasts. They are called the Sierra Madre Occidental and the Sierra Madre Oriental. A famous Mexican writer once compared the two ranges to braids flowing from the head of an Indian girl and draping across the country.

Between the two mountain ranges lies a broad, relatively flat, Central Plateau. The Central Plateau is Mexico's largest land area. Most of the population and all of the biggest cities are found there. At its lowest point, the Central Plateau is still more than 4,000 feet (1,219 meters) above sea level. This altitude gives the plateau a gentle climate. However, the Central Plateau is plagued by a lack of rainfall. Much of it is desert. Farmers grow corn on the plateau, but risk disaster if the summer rains fail to fall.

There are many active and extinct volcanoes in Mexico. One was born in 1943, almost under the feet of a terrified farmer. It grew to a height of 1,700 feet (518 meters) and destroyed several villages. A volcano called Chinchon exploded in 1982. Volcanoes and earthquakes have terrorized Mexicans since ancient times. In September 1985, two earthquakes in south central Mexico killed about 10,000 people and destroyed many large buildings in Mexico City. Some people buried under rubble for more than a week were rescued.

Mexico is an especially long country. The distance down the Pacific Coast from its northern to its southern boundary is almost the same as the distance from New York to San Francisco. The weather does not necessarily get warmer as one goes south. In Mexico the mountains, not the latitudes, determine the climate. The temperatures are colder in the higher altitudes and warmer in

Ixtacihuatl Volcano southeast of Mexico City (above) is only one of the countless volcanoes in Mexico. Much of the Central Plateau (below) is plagued by a lack of rainfall.

Visitors to the sunny resort city of Acapulco on the Pacific coast bask in
year-round warmth. The daring divers who plunge from El Mirador (the diving
rock, above) into the shallow waters of the cove below awe those who watch.

the lower altitudes. It could be said that Mexico is a vertical, not a horizontal, country.

The Mexican lower altitudes are sometimes called *tierras calientes* (hot lands), while the higher altitudes are called *tierras frias* (cold lands). The world-famous beach resort of Acapulco lies at sea level on the Pacific coast. In January the average temperature in Acapulco is a sunny 78 degrees Fahrenheit (25.6 degrees Celsius). Mexico City is on the Central Plateau, about 7,000 feet (2,134 meters) above sea level. There a bucket of water left outside overnight in January can freeze. But in the so-called cold lands, the sun is warm during the day. At noon in Mexico City one is comfortable wearing a T-shirt outside even in the middle of January.

To the south, the Yucatán Peninsula juts into the Gulf of Mexico. Most of the peninsula lies in the tierras calientes. In the north, the Yucatán is dry, but farther south, the land is a tangle of steaming jungle. Exotic wild animals such as the jaguar still roam there.

A drive through Mexico from north to south is a spellbinding journey. A traveler sees hundreds of miles of lonely seacoast dotted by tiny fishing villages. He climbs mountains to green lands where spring seems eternal. Still higher, he crosses dizzying mountain peaks that might be covered with snow. Down the mountains heading inland spread rocky deserts. Finally the trip ends in thick, tropical jungle.

THE PEOPLE

In Mexico, Columbus Day is a very important holiday. Statues of Christopher Columbus stand in all of the cities and most of the

This statue of Christopher Columbus on El Paseo de la Reforma in Mexico City honors the man Mexicans consider to symbolize the birth of their race. Though the majority of Mexicans are mestizos (a mixture of European and Indian ancestry), the children singing the Mexican national anthem show the variety of the country's racial heritage.

small towns. To Mexicans, the famous sea captain symbolizes the birth of their race. Mexicans call Columbus Day *Dia de la Raza* (Day of the Race).

The dominant Mexican race is a blending of the Old World and the New World. Almost five hundred years ago, Europeans came from Spain, married the Indians, and created a new race called the *mestizos.* Mestizos are a mixture of white European and native Indian bloodlines. There are many pure Indians and whites in the country, too. There are also blacks and Asians. But the overwhelming majority of Mexicans call themselves mestizos.

Much of Mexican history has been a power struggle among the mestizos, the Indians, and the whites. That power struggle continues even today. Whites often boast of their "pure Spanish bloodlines." Mestizos feel superior to Indians. And Indians look upon whites as invaders and mestizos as mongrels.

Particularly puzzling to the foreigner is the rivalry between Indians and mestizos. The physical differences between the two are slight. White Mexicans sometimes say that being an Indian is really more a state of mind than it is a state of race. They consider Indians to be people who live in isolated areas, are poor, and use Indian expressions in their conversations. In their complicated scheme of classification, a mestizo can be considered an Indian, and a wealthy Indian can become a mestizo. Successful Indians sometimes whisper to their friends, "You know, I *used* to be an Indian."

RELIGION, LANGUAGE, AND FAMILY

Whether they claim to be mestizo, Indian, or white, over 90 percent of Mexicans are Roman Catholic. No law requires this, as the government has allowed religious freedom, with a few certain restrictions. In years past the clergy were forbidden to vote or own property. Religious activities were banned in schools. But these laws were not always enforced. Still, Mexicans traditionally have remained dedicated Catholics. In 1991 Mexico's legislature passed constitutional amendments to end these restrictions. When Pope John Paul II visited in 1979 millions flocked to Mexico City to see him. A strange hush fell over the nation when he spoke, as everyone seemed to crowd around a radio or television to listen. When United States President Jimmy Carter visited a few weeks later only politicians and a few others greeted him. No one could create the same excitement as the pope, whom Mexicans call *"el Papa."*

When the Spaniards first arrived in Mexico, they discovered a country where the people spoke dozens of different languages. As the mestizo race developed, the Spanish language spread. Still, many pockets of Indian people resisted learning Spanish. As late as 1970, it was estimated that some one million Mexicans spoke only their ancient, tribal language. In recent years, however, radio and television have spread to homes in the most remote villages. Now only a few old people cannot speak Spanish. Mexican children growing up in Indian areas sometimes call the tribal words they hear "Grandma's tongue."

To a Mexican, nothing is more important than the family. Earthquakes or volcanoes can destroy everything, but if family members are unharmed, a Mexican will thank God for His blessings. Insulting a family member, even in the smallest way, is the most dangerous mistake an outsider can make in talking to a Mexican.

Who rules the family is, like so much about Mexican society, complicated. Outwardly, it appears that the father is supreme boss. For ages, Mexican women were subservient to men. They were not even allowed to vote in presidential elections until 1958. In the family structure, however, women only *seem* to play a minor role. The father is the one who normally announces an important decision in the family. But that decision is made only after a long, closed-door discussion with the mother.

Strong family bonds produce marvelously well-behaved and happy children. Mexican children grow up with a blend of discipline and love. Rarely are they bratty or withdrawn. Writer Charles Flandrau once mused that all the world's children ought to be required to be Mexican until age fifteen.

Trying to understand the Mexican character is difficult. Even Mexicans find this to be true. Among themselves, Mexicans love to discuss and marvel at their own behavior. Mexican writer Ramón Xirau once said, "The Mexican questions the sense of his

To a Mexican, nothing is more important than the family, and strong family bonds produce happy, well-behaved children.

own being, of his own nature. Who else wonders about the meaning of his own existence?"

But there is a key to puzzling out the fascinating world of Mexican society. That key is the study of its past.

A RICH AND EXCITING HISTORY

Few nations have a more exciting past than Mexico. As might be expected, contrasts and complications abound in its history. The story of Mexico is bloody yet glorious. The national leaders have been either saintlike heroes or the lowliest of villains. The people have passed laws, broken laws, waged war, and made peace.

*At the Plaza of Three Cultures in Mexico City (above), the ruins of an
ancient Aztec pyramid, a Spanish colonial church, and a modern glass and steel
housing complex represent three distinct periods in the history of Mexico.*

Near the broad Mexico City boulevard called *El Paseo de la
Reforma* lies a most unusual plaza. It is called *La Plaza de Tres
Culturas* (the Plaza of Three Cultures). Historians often divide
Mexican history into three periods: the ancient period (before the
coming of the Spaniards), the colonial period (while the Spaniards
ruled), and the modern period (after Mexico achieved its
independence). In the plaza, a visitor can see architecture from all
three periods in an area about the size of a football field. On one
side of the plaza are the ruins of an ancient pyramid. On the
opposite side is a faded gray church built by the Spaniards.
Towering over both structures is a modern glass and steel housing
complex. Nowhere else in the nation do the three historic periods
come together as neatly as they do in the Plaza of Three Cultures.
It is a perfect place to begin the study of the story of Mexico.

Chapter 2

ANCIENT MEXICO

Man is a comparative latecomer to Mexico. Archaeologists believe that human beings began to roam northern Mexico about 40,000 B.C. About 3000 B.C. the ancient Mexicans discovered how to grow and harvest maize (corn). This led to the establishment of farming villages.

Rugged mountains and thick jungles made communication difficult between the far-flung villages. Because of these natural barriers, many separate cultures developed. But several aspects of life in Indian Mexico were shared by all of the people. Maize was the staple food for everyone. Indian people later told their Spanish conquerors that ancient gods had taught them how to plant and harvest maize. Mexico had no large animals such as horses or oxen that could be trained to pull carts. Consequently, Mexicans never invented or learned to use the wheel or the plow. Also, Mexicans never discovered iron, although they did use copper, tin, and lead. Finally, all Mexican Indian cultures practiced some form of human sacrifice. The common belief was that gods could be satisfied only by the ritualistic killing of human beings.

Advanced civilizations never developed in northern Mexico. Rainfall was too scant there to support a large, agricultural

This massive stone head was carved by Olmec sculptors.

society. To the south, however, lay a fertile region that geographers now call Mesoamerica. The region includes the Central Plateau and spreads south to what is today Central America. In ancient Mesoamerica some remarkable civilizations developed.

THE OLMEC

The first high civilization to develop in Mesoamerica was that of the Olmec. They lived along the Gulf of Mexico near what is today the state of Veracruz. The Olmec civilization lasted from about 1200 to 100 B.C. The Olmec people built cities, developed an early calendar, and used a hieroglyphic written language.

Little is known about everyday life among the Olmec, but their art has endured. Olmec sculptors carved massive stone heads of men with strangely staring eyes. Heads have been found that stand over 9 feet (2.7 meters) tall and weigh 40 tons (36 metric

This painted ceramic whistle in the form of a fat god was made by a Maya sculptor.

MAYA
EMPIRE

tons). The heads are moon-shaped, with such strikingly Negroid features that some historians believe there must have been contact between the Olmec and the ancient people of Africa. The Olmec also fashioned fine jade jewelry. They may have worshipped the jaguars that roamed their jungle country because they made jade figures with human bodies and snarling jaguar heads.

THE MAYA

Probably the most brilliant of all the ancient people in Mesoamerica were the Maya. Their civilization flourished in southern Mexico and Central America.

The Maya were a mysterious people. No one knows where they came from or how and when they established their civilization. Many historians believe the Maya adapted their culture from the Olmec. Others claim the Maya developed entirely on their own,

*The once-magnificent Maya city of Palenque
in the state of Chiapas now lies in ruins.*

but at a very rapid rate. A few writers speculate that the Maya were the descendants of a lost civilization such as the legendary land of Atlantis.

The Maya left one puzzling clue as to the start of their culture. The curious date 3114 B.C. marks the beginning of the Maya calendar. Most persons in the Western world base the calendar on the birth of Christ. What earthshaking event could have happened to the Maya in 3114 B.C.? According to historians, Maya culture had not even begun to emerge at that time. The significance of the beginning of their calendar is a mystery the ancient Maya took to their graves.

During the period from A.D. 200 to 800, Maya civilization reached its zenith. Their population numbered some two million. They built magnificent cities such as Palenque and Tikal. The ruins of many Maya cities have been excavated and can be visited today. Probably scores more lie hidden in the jungle, overgrown with vines, still undiscovered.

Far left: A Maya manuscript
Left: A Maya wood carving of a seated dignitary or priest

No people in all the ancient world were more obsessed with the passage of time than were the Maya. The calendar they devised was more accurate than any calendar used up to the modern era. Maya priests divided time into certain periods. Each period was influenced by one of their gods. Since some gods were good and others evil, different periods of time became lucky or unlucky. There was a lucky time to plant maize and a lucky time to harvest it. Farmers sought the advice of priests before making major decisions.

Religion dominated the lives of the ancient Maya. They worshipped a wind god, a rain god, a soil god, and a host of others. The sun and moon were held to be sacred; the Maya believed that both man and the gods came from those two heavenly bodies. To this day, the Maya language calls the moon "our mother" and the sun "our father."

This observatory at Chichen Itzá was used by Maya astronomers.

To communicate with their gods the Maya studied the stars. Their priests were both astronomers and mathematicians. Without the help of computers or telescopes, they plotted the course of heavenly bodies with astonishing accuracy. Fifteen hundred years ago, Maya priests drew the path of the planet Venus with such precision that modern computers say they were off only fourteen seconds a year.

Sometime around A.D. 850, the Maya stopped building great cities. The Maya civilization, which had been expanding since its birth, mysteriously died. A new Maya culture emerged years later, but the unique brilliance of the old Maya disappeared forever. Historians are still unsure of the reasons for the culture's sudden decline. Perhaps it is only fitting that the society of these brilliant people should end the way it started—shrouded in mystery.

The Zapotec people flattened an entire mountaintop in what is today the state of Oaxaca to accommodate Monte Albán, their religious center (above).

THE GOLDEN AGE OF MESOAMERICA

Historians call the period of Mesoamerican history between the years A.D. 300 and 900 the Classical Period or the Golden Age. It was an era when magnificent cities rose from the Maya lands in the south to the mountains and plateaus in the north.

In what is today the state of Oaxaca, people of the Zapotec culture built Monte Albán. They flattened an entire mountaintop to accommodate their religious center, which included colossal pyramids and temples. Trying to conceive how this grand city was built staggers the imagination. All the building materials—and food and water for the workers—had to be pulled up a sheer mountain wall.

Feathered serpent heads representing the Aztec god Quetzalcóatl and images of the round-eyed rain god Tláloc decorate the pyramid of Quetzalcóatl in Teotihuacán.

Starting about A.D. 100, an even greater city began to rise some thirty miles from present-day Mexico City. Exactly what culture built the city is unknown. But when the Aztec first saw the thousand-year-old city, they refused to believe it had been built by men. Instead, they thought it had been made by giants. They named the great city Teotihuacán, meaning "Where Men Become Gods."

The civilization at Teotihuacán reached its height around the sixth century A.D. At that time, the city covered 8 square miles (20.7 square kilometers) and held some 150,000 people. Quite probably it was the largest city anywhere in the world. Dominating the skyline was the 200-foot-tall (61 meters) Pyramid of the Sun. It is almost as large as the famous Cheops pyramid in

Egypt. From the Pyramid of the Sun spread lesser pyramids and hundreds of homes. The civilization of Teotihuacán was so powerful that it influenced the Maya culture far to the south.

City building was not the only accomplishment in Mesoamerica during its Golden Age. Farming became scientific and knowledge of astronomy and mathematics soared. Ancient Mexicans achieved excellence in sculpture, painting, and dozens of crafts. The people of Mesoamerica also must have developed a high form of law. War was waged in ancient Mexico, but there seemed to be little conflict during the Golden Age. Instead, wall paintings of that period show a people more interested in science and the arts than in warfare.

There were startling differences between the Old World and the New World during Mexico's Classical Period. At that time, Europe was suffering though the Dark Ages. Knowledge in the Old World actually retrogressed as European scholars gradually forgot what had been learned from the advanced civilizations of Greece and Rome. What if the two cultures had met when Europe was at its nadir and Mexico at its zenith? Who would have conquered whom? How would world history have been changed? These are some of the questions that make history such a fascinating study.

For unknown reasons, the Golden Age declined in the eighth century A.D. and ended in the ninth. The Classical Period terminated suddenly and mysteriously. Perhaps a change in climate destroyed the agriculture of the advanced civilizations. Perhaps the once peaceful people began engaging in destructive wars.

The end of the Classical Period marked a turning point in the history of ancient Mexico. What followed was shockingly different from the old order.

AZTEC
EMPIRE

Tenochtítlan

THE AZTEC

In the Central Plateau lies the fertile Valley of Mexico. It is 60 miles (96.5 kilometers) long and 40 miles (64.3 kilometers) wide. Present-day Mexico City is at the southern tip of the valley. Before the coming of the Spaniards, glistening lakes dotted the valley's floor. After the Classical Period, the valley became Mexico's heartland. Whoever controlled it controlled the country.

In the 900s, a people called the Toltec ruled the Valley of Mexico. The Toltec were a mighty race of warriors and builders. For almost four hundred years they kept a steel grip on an empire that included all of northern Mesoamerica. But starting in the 1200s, a rival group of people came out of the barbarian north. They hungered for a homeland and for power.

According to their own legends, the Aztec once lived in seven caves located in the mountains northwest of the Valley of Mexico. While there they began worshipping a god named Huitzilopóchtli. He was an eternally angry god whose raging temper could be soothed only by human blood.

The angry god ordered the Aztec to leave their caves and seek a new home. So, carrying a statue of their god on a portable altar, the Aztec began a long journey. Their traditions claim the trek lasted more than a hundred years. The Aztec crossed mountains and deserts. Finally they entered the Valley of Mexico where they encountered advanced tribes and marveled at the vast stone cities.

This statue in Mexico City commemorates the Aztec legend of the founding of Tenochtítlan.

In the valley their god spoke. He ordered the people to search until they found an eagle sitting on a cactus while eating a snake. At that place they must build a mighty city of their own. On an island in Lake Texcóco, the Aztec saw an eagle sitting on a cactus with a snake dangling from its beak. Their long search was over. They began to construct a city they called Tenochtítlan. It became a city so dazzling that when the Spaniards first saw it they thought they were dreaming.

The Aztec devoted as much attention to the rigors of warfare as the people of the Golden Age had devoted to the study of science and the arts. By the 1400s, the mighty Aztec army had carved out an empire that stretched from the Gulf of Mexico to the Pacific Ocean and almost as far south as present-day Guatemala.

A model of the Aztec island city of Tenochtítlan is shown in the background. In front is a model of the main city square at the time. The Templo Mayor, now being excavated in Mexico City, is the large, two-part structure with the twin temples on top.

Obeying the wishes of their angry god, the Aztec built their capital city in the middle of Lake Texcóco. When completed, the island city spread over 20 square miles (51.8 square kilometers) and held some 100,000 people. Three broad causeways connected the city to the mainland. Its major streets were canals on which canoes loaded with goods were paddled to the city's markets. Scores of drawbridges spanned the canals. At the hub of the city rose massive flat-topped pyramids with temples on their crowns.

Rows of skulls lined up on racks below the pyramid of Huitzilopóchtli present grim evidence of the Aztec practice of human sacrifice.

Surrounding the pyramids were government buildings and palaces that housed the emperor, the nobles, and the priests. Beholding this great city, an Aztec poet wrote:

> The city is spread out in circles of jade,
> Radiating flashes of light...
> Beside it the lords are borne in boats;
> Over them extends a flowing mist.

The city's tallest pyramid was dedicated to the angry god Huitzilopóchtli. From the top of the pyramid, his statue brooded over all of Tenochtitlan. Below lay gruesome evidence of his demands. Lined up neatly on wooden racks were endless rows of human skulls.

Early in Aztec history, human sacrifice was a rare event in religious practice. But as the Aztec grew more powerful, their gods became more demanding. To soothe the gods, thousands of people were led to the grim sacrificial stone where priests cut out their hearts and flung them at the feet of the god's statue. Most of the victims were prisoners captured during battles with neighboring tribes. Indeed, a major reason the Aztec waged war was to capture sacrificial victims.

This stone serpent head representing the Aztec god Quetzalcóatl is one of many that decorated the base of the great temple at Tenochtítlan.

The second tallest pyramid in the Aztec capital was dedicated to an entirely different god. He was a kind, loving god named Quetzalcóatl. This kind god was worshipped by many other cultures in Mesoamerica. According to legend, he once lived among the people and taught them medicine and farming. Above all, the gentle god told the people that human sacrifice was an evil practice. He preferred gifts of butterflies rather than bloody human hearts. One day a rival god drove the gentle god out of Mexico. Quetzalcóatl supposedly disappeared to the east riding on a winged serpent. Before leaving, he vowed to return someday and rule all of Mexico. He even announced the date on which he would return. This vow would later be remembered by Aztec leaders at a critical time in their history.

In the year 1502, a warrior named Montezuma became emperor of the Aztec world. At the time, Aztec power was at its height. But strangers from an unheard-of land began to approach the shores of Mexico. They sailed ships bigger than a thousand Aztec war canoes. No ancient Mexican could possibly foresee the profound impact those strangers would have on their country.

Chapter 3

THREE CENTURIES OF SPANISH RULE

Mystery and magic obsessed the Aztec leader Montezuma. He worshipped all the gods and feared the power they wielded over people. Like most Aztec, Montezuma interpreted strange events to be warnings from the gods. Suddenly his empire was besieged by unusual happenings. Messengers running relays from the coast claimed that curious vessels, "mountains that moved on the sea," had been spotted in the Gulf of Mexico. Also, eerie signs appeared in the sky. In 1517, a three-headed comet hung over the Valley of Mexico. Montezuma's astronomers could not explain it. For forty nights, an unknown light burned on the eastern horizon. In a distant battlefield, a general claimed that his troops had been defeated when thousands of stones suddenly rained from the sky.

Montezuma's priests warned him to beware of the year *Ce Acatl*, or One Reed. In that year, the great god Quetzalcóatl had promised to return to Mexico. The year One Reed on the Aztec calendar corresponded to the year 1519 on the European calendar.

THE SPANISH CONQUEST OF MEXICO

On Good Friday in 1519, a band of five hundred Spaniards landed at a natural harbor at what is today the city of Veracruz. They were adventurers seeking riches who had sailed from their outpost in Cuba. The Spaniards were driven by rumors of cities with buildings of solid gold and rivers that flowed liquid silver.

While probing the Mexican coast, the Spaniards were attacked by Indian warriors. But the strangers had weapons the Indians had never dreamed could exist. Their iron armor repelled native arrows. Their thundering muskets could kill a warrior from a distance of 50 yards (45.7 meters). Finally, the Spaniards had horses. To the natives, they seemed like supernatural beasts. At first, the Indians believed the horse and rider to be one being.

Leading the Spaniards was a fearless and brilliant soldier named Hernando Cortés. After he defeated the coastal tribes, Cortés demanded gold. The people pointed inland and told him that mountains of gold could be found in a place they called *Mejico*. Mejico was the coastal people's name for the city of Tenochtítlan.

A determined Cortés ordered his men to march inland. Before leaving the coast, Cortés set fire to his small fleet of ships. That way he could add the crewmen to his ranks. And his men would be unable to rebel and flee to Cuba if the march inland became dangerous.

News of Cortés's march quickly reached Montezuma. He was told of "thunder sticks" and "giant dogs of war." The invaders had white skin and hair on their faces. According to some Aztec legends, the god Quetzalcóatl was a bearded white man. The strangers came out of the east in the year One Reed. Quetzalcoatl had left Mexico to the east and vowed to return in the year One

Reed. The invaders preached a new religion to the coastal people. They claimed that human sacrifice was an evil practice. Quetzalcóatl also condemned human sacrifice. Certainly the leader of the invaders was Quetzalcóatl himself. How was Montezuma, a mere mortal, supposed to deal with a god?

As the Spaniards marched closer, Montezuma issued puzzling and contradictory orders. First he sent emissaries offering gifts of gold if Cortés and his men would only go away. Seeing the gold, however, only whetted the Spaniards' thirst for more. Then Montezuma ordered his subject tribes to attack the advancing Spaniards. But the invaders beat back every attack. Finally, Montezuma ordered hundreds of victims to the sacrificial stone beneath the statue of the angry god Huitzilopóchtli. Still the Spaniards continued their advance.

By November, 1519, Cortés and his men entered the Valley of Mexico. Upon seeing Tenochtítlan, Cortés wrote, "The magnificence, the strange and marvelous things of this great city, [were] so remarkable as not to be believed."

On a causeway leading into the city, Cortés and Montezuma met and exchanged gifts. Each was in awe of the other. Cortés was overwhelmed by the majesty of the Aztec empire. Montezuma believed he was meeting a god. For the next few days, the Spaniards and Indians lived together peacefully; but trouble soon developed.

While making a courtesy visit to the Aztec palace, the bold Cortés suddenly seized Montezuma and held him prisoner. The Aztec people, believing Cortés to be a god, did not react. Months dragged by while the Spaniards held Montezuma and hoarded all the gold they could find. Gradually, the Aztec realized that the Spaniards were not gods as they had once believed. In June, 1520, the Aztec revolted and drove the foreigners out of their city. While trying to swim across Lake Texcóco, many Spaniards drowned, weighted down by the gold they had stashed in their packs.

Cortés fumed at the defeat and vowed to retake the city. He had learned that the Aztec were hated by neighboring tribes because they constantly demanded tributes of gold and sacrificial victims. Cortés recruited those tribes to march with him against the Aztec. Also, more Spaniards had arrived on the coast and Cortés persuaded them to join his ranks. Soon Cortés commanded nine hundred heavily armed Spaniards and thousands of Indian warriors. The wily Cortés even built a fleet to sail across Lake Texcóco and storm the shores of the Aztec capital.

In the spring of 1521, Cortés's forces assaulted Tenochtítlan. A furious battle raged for four months. The canals of the island city became blackened with dead soldiers. In the end, the relentless, driving Cortés defeated the Aztec. Thousands of people had been killed. The marvelous city of Tenochtítlan was in ruins.

The bloody battle marked a new period in Mexican history. It was the beginning of the merging of the Old World with the New World. Today, a monument in Mexico City marks the site where the last skirmish in the battle was fought. A placard proclaims, "It was neither triumph nor defeat—it was instead the painful birth of the mestizo people who are Mexico today."

Opposite: In November of 1519, a few months after Hernando Cortés had arrived on the shores of Mexico, Aztec emperor Montezuma and Cortés met and exchanged gifts on a causeway leading into the city of Tenochtítlan.

THE INITIAL RESULTS OF THE CONQUEST

From their base in the Valley of Mexico, Cortés and his officers marched in every direction. Other bands of soldiers called *conquistadores* (conquerors) sailed from Spain and swept over the New World. Most of the conquistadores were adventurers who dreamed of making overnight fortunes by plundering Indian gold. They regarded the Indian people as heathens whom they could enslave, steal from, and kill without guilt. Hernando Cortés, called cruel by some historians, was saintly compared to the conquistadores who came after him.

As soon as they took power, the Spaniards forbade the Indians to practice human sacrifice. Even the bloodiest of the conquistadores cited human sacrifice as proof that the Indians were godless pagans. But it should be noted that the invaders had grown up during the horrors of the Spanish Inquisition. They had seen people tortured and burned at the stake, supposedly in the name of God. The Indians, on the other hand, had no concept of torture. And they were appalled when they learned that the Spaniards burned people alive.

The Spanish search for quick fortunes in Mexico proved disappointing. Though Mexico had vast deposits of gold and silver, most of that wealth was still in the ground waiting to be mined. Gold and silver were not used as money by the native people. Therefore, the Indians had never mined the minerals on a large scale.

With scant gold to distribute, the conquistador leaders paid their men in grants of land. That the land once belonged to the Indians made little difference to the conquistadores. Ordinary soldiers were given ranches one hundred times larger than farms they could hope to acquire in Spain. Officers received huge grants of land called *encomiendas*. Cortés himself owned an encomienda that spread over 25,000 square miles (64,750 square kilometers). An encomienda owner controlled the land *and* the Indian people living on his property. A typical encomienda deed read, "Unto you are given in trust [a certain number] of Indians for you to make use of in your farm and mines." The Indians who resisted this enslavement were killed by their new overlords.

The establishment of encomiendas began a system of land-ownership that haunted Mexico for the next four hundred years. It led to the enormous gap between the rich and poor that still exists. Even today, many rich and powerful Mexicans owe their fortunes to a long-ago conquistador ancestor. José López Portillo, who was president of Mexico from 1976 to 1982, traced his family's roots back to one of Cortés's original five hundred soldiers. Before he became president, his family was one of the richest in Mexico. By the time he left office, López Portillo was one of the richest men in the world.

Forever hungry for gold, the Spaniards explored their new empire. In only twenty years, they trekked as far south as present-day El Salvador and as far north as present-day Kansas in the United States. The explorers claimed the new land for the Spanish king and called it New Spain.

The Spaniards were energetic builders. From the ruins of old Tenochtítlan they constructed a new capital city. Often they used the bricks of the wrecked pyramids to build houses, government buildings, and churches. They called the new capital Mexico City.

In agriculture, the Spaniards brought vast changes to the New World. They introduced pigs and cattle, and mules and horses to ease farm work. The Europeans planted oranges and limes that

Ever since the early Spaniards planted citrus fruits,
Mexicans have been able to enjoy oranges and limes as well as
pineapples, bananas, and other fruits native to their country.

later flourished in the sunny land. Today, the mountains of citrus fruits stacked up in the markets make it hard to imagine Mexico without oranges. In turn, the Indians gave the Spaniards tomatoes, corn, chocolate, and peanuts. The Spaniards also developed what proved to be a harmful habit when they took to smoking what the Indians called tobacco.

But the Spaniards brought with them the devastating disease of smallpox as well. Smallpox had been common in Europe for generations, and white men had developed an immunity to the point where the disease no longer killed them in large numbers. The Indians of the New World, however, had no such immunity. Smallpox swept over New Spain, killing Indians by the hundreds of thousands.

The most profound result of the painful meeting between the two cultures was the introduction of Christianity to the New World. Traveling at the heels of the conquistadores were black-robed Catholic priests. A few were as hungry for power as the conquistadores were for gold. However, most were gentle men who took seriously their vows to live in poverty and humility and to win new souls for Christ. Many priests were outraged by the cruelties their countrymen inflicted on the Indians.

The priests found the Indian people eager listeners when they spoke of a Christian God. Accepting a new god was easy for the natives since they believed in the existence of many gods.

Many Indians converted to Christianity following a strange and still unexplainable event that occurred near Mexico City.

THE VIRGIN OF GUADALUPE

What follows is a story all Mexicans grow up with. It is a miraculous tale, and most Mexican people believe it to be entirely true.

In January, 1531, an Indian man climbed a hill in the town of Guadalupe Hidalgo, about three miles north of Mexico City. He was a newly baptized Christian and had taken the name Juan Diego. Near the top of the hill, Juan Diego heard sweet music. Then a woman's voice called his name. Juan suddenly saw a woman who looked "as radiant as the sun." Certainly the woman was a saint. But unlike the pictures of the saints he had seen in the Spanish church, this woman had dark skin much like his own.

The woman told Juan Diego to go to Mexico City and speak to the bishop. She wanted a church to be built on the top of the hill so she could be close to her people. When Juan asked who she was, the woman answered, "I am the mother of all of you who dwell in this land."

Juan hurried to Mexico City to see the bishop.

The Catholic bishop was a Spaniard named Zumarraga. He was one of the many priests who were horrified by his countrymen's treatment of the Indians. But when Bishop Zumarraga met with the breathless and excited Juan Diego, he simply could not believe the wild story. So Juan Diego sadly returned to the village of Guadalupe Hidalgo. There the woman urged him to seek a second audience with the bishop. This time Juan Diego fell to his knees in front of the bishop, and with tears streaming down his face repeated what he had seen.

Bishop Zumarraga told Juan to ask the woman for some token to prove she was sent to Mexico by God. Again Juan returned to the hill. The woman said he should return the next day.

When Juan Diego returned, the woman took him to a spot where a delicate rosebush grew out of the rocky soil. Juan was astonished. Only cactus plants grew on this hill. Juan picked the roses and placed them under his cape (*tilma*). He then raced to Mexico City. Surely these roses were the evidence needed to convince the bishop that this woman was sent by God.

At the bishop's palace, Juan opened his tilma. The roses fell to the floor. "These flowers are the miracle you asked to see," Juan blurted out. "Never before, not in a thousand years, have roses grown on Tepeyac Hill."

Strangely, the bishop did not look at the roses. Instead he gazed at the inside of Juan's tilma. Painted there was a masterful picture of the woman Juan had seen on the hill. No one—not Juan Diego, not Bishop Zumarraga, nor anyone else in New Spain—could explain how the portrait got there.

What reasonable explanation can be offered for this event which the Catholic church later recognized as a miracle? Some historians believe it was a hoax dreamed up by Bishop Zumarraga. They say the bishop commissioned an artist to paint the picture so he could convince the Spaniards that the Indian people were favored by God. That way he hoped the Spaniards would stop mistreating them. But experts agree that the picture was so masterfully painted that no artist living in New Spain at the time could have produced it.

Today the old town of Guadalupe Hidalgo is a neighborhood in sprawling Mexico City. The miraculous picture painted on the coarse cloth of the tilma still hangs over a church altar there. Mexicans travel hundreds of miles to pray before it. And in practically every Mexican home there is a framed picture or a statue of the Virgin of Guadalupe. In a poor man's home the statue is made of straw. In a rich man's home the statue is made of ivory, with perhaps a touch of gold. But for all Mexicans, the miraculous lady remains *Our* Lady of Guadalupe.

The National Cathedral in Mexico City (above) is one of twelve thousand churches built under Spanish rule. Left: This Spanish colonial building with graceful arches, once a convent, is now a fine arts institute.

THE COLONY OF NEW SPAIN

For three centuries the Spanish banner flew over Mexico City. New Spain made some significant achievements.

The architecture of New Spain was a delightful blend of the Old World and the New. Spanish buildings with graceful arches took on the color and the airiness of the new land. Twelve thousand churches were built under Spanish rule. Their towering spires still dominate colonial towns. Mexico City became the handsomest city in the Western Hemisphere. European travelers marveled at its broad, tree-lined streets, its fountains, and its parks.

Spanish power also brought peace to the warring people of preconquest Mexico. The Spanish authorities would not permit intertribal warfare. Not since the ancient Golden Age had the people enjoyed such freedom from wars.

However, Spanish rule did create a rigid class system that was based on race. Three major races—white, mestizo, and Indian—lived in New Spain. By 1800, Indians comprised about 60 percent of the population. Most were landless peasants living under the yoke of white overlords. The mestizo population had grown to about two million in 1800, and even then it seemed certain that they would soon absorb the pure Indian and pure white races. The mestizos lived a step higher than the Indians, but felt frustrated because everything they longed for was already owned by whites. During the colonial period, some three hundred thousand Spanish whites immigrated to New Spain. Those who arrived earliest claimed the best land. Rich whites lived in a splendor rivaling that of European kings and queens.

But wealth in New Spain did not mean political power. The Spanish court realized that wealthy, educated colonists would be likely to demand independence. So the whites were divided into two classes: the *creoles* (whites born in New Spain) and the *gachupínes* (whites born in European Spain). The Spanish king insisted the colony be ruled only by gachupín officials loyal to the Spanish throne. A Spanish viceroy once told his creole subjects, "For once and all, know that you have been born to be silent and to obey, and neither to discuss nor to hold opinions on the affairs of government."

In the late 1700s, parts of the world began to rumble with revolutions and dreams of new societies. In France, the peasants rose up against oppressive landowners. In America, a colonial people broke their ties with England. Slowly these ideas crept into the minds of people in New Spain. In 1800, the word *independence* was being whispered on the streets. A decade later, the whispers became a roar.

The church at Dolores Hidalgo where independence was declared

Chapter 4

INDEPENDENCE
AND TURMOIL

Often great historical movements begin by accident rather than by design. Such was the case with the Mexican War of Independence. The war started by chance, and was led by a very unlikely soldier.

THE WAR OF INDEPENDENCE

Father Miguel Hidalgo y Castilla was a kindhearted, bookish priest who served in the town of Dolores about 150 miles (241 kilometers) north of Mexico City. He was a creole in an Indian parish, but was loved by his people. Father Hidalgo was also a member of a discussion group made up of educated creoles. The prime subject of the group's talk was independence for Mexico.

Spanish authorities, long suspicious of Father Hidalgo, issued an order to arrest each member of the group. An informant warned Hidalgo of the coming arrests. The group had made plans to rise up against Spain, but those plans were two months away from action. Now, under the threat of arrest, Hidalgo had to act immediately.

*Father Miguel Hidalgo
y Castilla (left)
began the war for
Mexican independence.*

At daybreak on September 16, 1810, Father Hidalgo rang his church bell as if summoning his Indian parishioners to Mass. When the people had gathered in the churchyard, he uttered the *Grito de Dolores* (Cry of Dolores). It is the most famous speech in Mexican history. According to tradition, he used the words, "Mexicans! Viva Mexico! Viva independence! Viva the Virgin of Guadalupe!" Also according to tradition, the Indian people of Dolores echoed each one of his "vivas" and shouted back, "Death to the gachupínes!"

A revolution began without plan, without policy, and practically without weapons.

Carrying clubs, knives, and a few ancient rifles, the rebels began a grand march toward Mexico City. The leaders carried a banner bearing a picture of the Virgin of Guadalupe. Under her protection, many marchers believed they could not be harmed. Later, a few of Hidalgo's men tried to jam Spanish artillery by holding straw sombreros over the mouths of cannons.

In the rich silver-mining city of Guanajuato, gachupín officials and Spanish soldiers barricaded themselves in a thick-walled granary and waited for the rebels. A terrible battle broke out. Spanish artillery and rifle fire cut down Hidalgo's men by the hundreds. At the height of the battle, an Indian mine worker—who would forever be a hero in Mexican history—crept up to the wooden door of the granary and set it on fire. Hidalgo's men poured through and overwhelmed the Spaniards.

That night, Indian and mestizo soldiers sacked the town and hacked Spaniards to death in the streets. Hidalgo and other revolutionary officers tried to stop the slaughter, but the floodgates of hatred had been opened. The Indians and mestizos seemed to want to avenge every crime committed by the Spaniards since the days of Cortés. The cobblestone streets of Guanajuato flowed red. Days passed before Hidalgo could restore order.

The rebels next fought and won a pitched battle on a mountaintop overlooking the capital. Mexico City lay before them. But at the last moment, Father Hidalgo ordered his men to turn back. Many historians believe the priest retreated because he feared a repeat of the bloodbath at Guanajuato.

During the long march back, thousands of Hidalgo's men deserted and others gave up in the face of Spanish ambushes. The Spanish army retook the city of Guanajuato. The rebel leaders—including Hidalgo—were arrested.

Father Hidalgo was tried, found guilty of treason, and shot by a firing squad. It is said that the parish priest, forgiving to the end, gave each member of his firing squad a piece of candy.

Despite the enormity of the defeat, Father Hidalgo had lighted the torch of Mexican independence. Soon the flame burned in

*This granary in Guanajuato (left) was the scene of the first revolutionary
victory in 1810. Ten years after Father Hidalgo's execution in 1811,
Mexico declared its independence. Now, every September 16,
flags bedeck Mexico City (right) during the Independence Day celebration.*

every corner of the country. Revolutionary armies continued to
fight. One was led by a mestizo priest named José María Morelos
y Pavón, another by an Indian officer named Vincente Guerrero.
In the Old World, Spain was weakened by constant European
wars. She could no longer afford to send troops and money to
fight the revolutionaries. In 1821, ten years after Hidalgo's
execution, Mexico was declared an independent nation.

WAR WITH THE UNITED STATES

Because Mexicans had little experience with self-government,
chaos and civil war plagued the country in the years following
independence. Generals and other strong men seized power and
proclaimed themselves president, only to be overthrown in a

In 1836, Mexican General Antonio López de Santa Anna and his troops won the battle at the fortress called the Alamo (left) in San Antonio, Texas.

matter of months. Complicating the new republic's problems were strained relations with its neighbor to the north.

When Mexico first achieved independence, it was a land giant comparable to today's Russia, China, or Brazil. Its borders included the present-day American states of Texas, New Mexico, Arizona, Nevada, Utah, California, and part of Colorado. However, much of the northern territory was sparsely settled and had little contact with Mexico City. For years, those nearly empty areas had been eyed by land-hungry Americans.

In 1836, American settlers living in the north broke away from Mexico and established a separate nation they called Texas. The Mexican government sent an army to bring the land back into its fold. The troops were led by a gloomy general named Antonio López de Santa Anna, who liked to boast, "I am the Napoleon of the West." In San Antonio, Santa Anna annihilated the American settlers in a bloody battle at a fortress called the Alamo.

The dispute over Texas led to the 1846 war with the United States. The United States Army attacked Mexico by marching across the Rio Grande in the north and by landing troops at Veracruz in the south.

Complicating the Mexican defense was the chaos in the capital. While the Americans were closing in, the Mexicans were busy changing presidents. General Santa Anna headed the intrigue. In a thirty-year period, Santa Anna became president of Mexico eleven separate times. Aided by the confusion in Mexico City, the American army overwhelmed the Mexican defenders.

The defeat was both humiliating and costly. Mexico lost its territory north of the Rio Grande. In all, 918,355 square miles (2,378,530 square kilometers) were ceded to the Americans. Gold was soon discovered in California, making its loss even more grievous. For generations, and to a certain extent even today, Mexicans have brooded over the defeat and the staggering loss of land.

BENITO JUÁREZ AND THE REFORM

One day in 1828, the mighty General Santa Anna stopped in a restaurant in the southern state of Oaxaca. A young Indian man served him. The Indian was a struggling college student so poor he could not even afford shoes. Santa Anna paid scant attention to the barefoot young man who waited on his table. But years later, the former waiter reminded the powerful general of their first, chance meeting. At the time, he was about to become president of Mexico. His name was Benito Juárez.

Juárez was the champion of the poor Indians and mestizos. Old-line Spanish families had clung stubbornly to their ranches,

Left: Monument to Benito Juárez, president of Mexico from 1857 to 1872. Right: Crowds gather at his birthplace.

banks, and mines. The Catholic church also had acquired land, money, and power. Juárez and his supporters hoped to change, or reform, the laws that kept a few landowners and church officials rich while millions of others lived in poverty. The reform movement ignited a civil war that raged for three years. Juárez became president in 1857, but the war over reform continued.

Meanwhile, in faraway France, an ambitious leader plotted to take advantage of the strife in Mexico. Mexico owed enormous sums of money to European banks. Napoleon III used those debts as an excuse to invade the country. The French leader dreamed of building an empire in the New World. But on May 5, 1862, his French army was soundly beaten by Mexican forces at the Battle of Puebla. Mexicans still celebrate this victory every fifth of May during the *Cinco de Mayo Fiesta*. Napoleon then sent a much larger army, and those soldiers swept into Mexico City a year later. President Benito Juárez was forced to flee to the United States.

Mexican history often reads like fiction. For that reason, dozens of novels and films have been based on the Mexico of old. The most romantic, yet tragic, of those stories concerns a charming young European couple who for a few short years ruled Mexico like an Old World king and queen.

MAXIMILIAN AND CARLOTA

Napoleon III turned to the noble Hapsburg family of Austria to provide an emperor for Mexico. He chose a handsome prince named Maximilian who was married to a ravishingly beautiful girl just out of her teens named Carlota. Napoleon III expected the couple to rule Mexico as his puppets. But the French leader was quickly surprised by their behavior.

Maximilian and his young wife fell in love with Mexico. Carlota had never seen so sunny a land with so many blooming flowers. Her favorite song became the haunting Mexican melody "La Paloma." Maximilian was impressed by the quiet strength of the Indian people. He hoped to become popular with the Indians and use that popularity as a base of power. The new emperor and empress ate Mexican food and wore Mexican clothes. In letters home they referred to themselves as "we Mexicans" and made scornful references to "you Europeans." Meanwhile, Napoleon III fumed at the young couple's sudden allegiance to Mexico.

As long as the French army occupied their country, the Mexican people were respectfully polite to Maximilian and Carlota. But they longed for their own President Juárez to return.

The tide turned for the French when the American Civil War ended. Having a European army at their back door violated American notions of the Monroe Doctrine. The American government gave Juárez money and arms to form a new army.

Napoleon III, who was disappointed over Maximilian's conduct in Mexico, ordered his army home. Maximilian and Carlota were shocked. They had come to Mexico intending to rule for life, not for only three years. Maximilian rounded up Mexican soldiers loyal to him, and prepared to fight Juárez. Carlota sailed to Europe to seek help. When the young couple kissed good-bye, they had no idea they would never see each other again.

Carlota went first to Paris to see Napoleon III. The French leader, ill and defeated, wept all through their talk. Next, Carlota traveled to Rome to speak with the pope. Her arduous travel and fears for her husband had begun to erode her mind. She told the pope that Napoleon III was trying to poison her. Finally, she went to her family home in Belgium. She refused to eat or drink anything during the journey for fear of being poisoned.

In Mexico, during a battle at the city of Querétaro, a Juárez army captured Maximilian. The emperor had opportunities to escape, but believed that running away would stain the dignity of his proud Hapsburg family. On June 19, 1867, Maximilian and two of his officers faced a firing squad. The Hapsburg prince stood at rigid attention in front of his executioners. Witnesses said that not one shiver swept his body before the shots rang out.

Upon hearing of her husband's death, Carlota entered a mental asylum where she remained until her death at age eighty-seven. She continued to love flowers and bright sunny days, and "La Paloma" remained her favorite song. In her old age, she often told her nurses that her husband was the "Sovereign of the Universe."

PORFIRIO DÍAZ AND DICTATORSHIP

A throng of cheering thousands greeted Benito Juárez as he reentered Mexico City riding in a black carriage. One of the cheering men was Porfirio Díaz, a trusted officer in Juárez's army. To him, the ideals of the Juárez reform laws were for dreamers. He had more practical notions of the aims of government.

Juárez died of a heart attack in 1872. His sudden death touched off a violent power struggle. Mexicans still had not established an orderly method of shifting power from one head of government to the next. In 1877 Porfirio Díaz became president. Except for a four-year period, he ruled until 1911.

Díaz believed that improvements in Mexico should start from the top and work their way down. He ignored the reform laws passed by Juárez. Although Díaz was a mestizo, he allowed the old white aristocracy to regain its land and power. By the end of the Díaz era, 90 percent of the rural people were landless, while half of the land area of Mexico was owned by some three thousand families.

For more than thirty years Díaz ruled Mexico the way a feudal lord might rule over a manor. Under his domination, many improvements were made. Railroads, many built by American companies, connected the major cities. Roads were improved and telephone and telegraph wires were strung. All these projects

For more than thirty years Porfirio Díaz (left) ruled Mexico like a dictator.

were completed because of Díaz's burning desire to make Mexico a modern country. But under his rule, the plight of the poor and landless peasant grew even more hopeless.

In 1910, Díaz invited world leaders to Mexico to celebrate the centennial of the War of Independence. But strange events began occurring, reminding some people of what had happened to the Aztec four hundred years earlier. The fiery Halley's comet burned in the night sky. The volcano at Colima erupted. Earthquakes shook the country. For many Mexicans, especially the Indians, these signs were dire warnings of profound changes that would soon wrack the land.

THE FALL OF THE DICTATORSHIP

In northern Mexico, a high-minded man named Francisco Madero wrote a pamphlet called "The Presidential Succession of 1910." He argued that the so-called elections that continually returned Díaz to office were phony. Díaz responded by throwing Madero into jail.

Pancho Villa (left) was one of many rebel leaders during the 1910-20 Revolution.

Madero was one of the wealthiest men in the country, but it was known that he fed the children of his farm workers at his own table. While he was in jail, peasant uprisings broke out in his support. In the north, they were led by a sometime cattle rustler named Pancho Villa. To the south, a farmer named Emiliano Zapata formed an army made up of tough Indian farm workers. In Mexico City, mobs rioting in front of the presidential palace demanded Madero's release.

Porfirio Díaz was eighty years old in 1910. Much of his government organization had grown rotten with age. Now it seemed as if a fire had broken out in Mexico, and the dictator was unable to extinguish it. After weeks of soul-searching, Díaz quietly resigned his office and slipped away to Europe.

In a free and honest election, Francisco Madero was elected president by an overwhelming vote. In the capital, bands played, boys beat on gasoline drums, and fireworks crackled in the night.

Madero was hailed as the champion of the poor and landless people. His election, the people believed, would mean peace and prosperity for all Mexicans.

But Mexico was entering a period of sleep that would be tortured by a nightmare. She would awaken in a modern age only after the nightmare had run its bloody course.

THE REVOLUTION OF 1910-20

From the start, Madero's government was under pressure by forces from the left and from the right. From the left, radical reformers urged him to break up the landed estates immediately and distribute the land to the peasants. From the right, the old aristocracy demanded that he protect property rights. Madero was an idealist who hoped to establish democracy and then let the people choose their own destiny. However, it was impossible to form a working democracy in a country where the majority lived in poverty and could not read or write.

Fifteen months after Madero took office, Mexico City was a battleground. Rival armies fought with cannons and machine guns over who would be first to challenge the Madero government.

Hoping to stop the fighting, Madero turned to a general named Victoriano Huerta. This was the president's gravest mistake. Huerta was a glutton for power. He used his army to seize Madero and later had him and the vice-president shot. Huerta then established a brutal dictatorship that lasted only eighteen months before he, too, was overthrown.

After Huerta, there began a confusing parade of presidents. From 1913 to 1920, ten different presidents ruled Mexico. Some held office for only a matter of weeks. One president held office for only forty-six minutes.

A constant civil war swept the land. Generals, hungry for power, recruited armies and fought one another. The entire population was pulled into the turmoil. Doctors and teachers found themselves fighting alongside mule tenders and shoemakers. Women and children followed their husbands and fathers into battle. When a man dropped, his wife or oldest child picked up his rifle and joined the melee. Casualties were so appalling that raw recruits became officers in a matter of days. A popular song told the story of a young soldier who entered battle at ten in the morning, became a lieutenant at eleven, a captain at noon, and "at ten minutes past noon a general of a division."

In the decade following 1910, the war reduced the population of Mexico by almost a million. One of every fifteen people in the country died. Some were killed in battle, and others died from the starvation and disease that followed the armies.

In that ten-year period, nearly all the major revolutionary leaders fought each other at one time or another. Obregón fought Villa; Villa fought Carranza; Carranza fought Calles; Zapata fought Gonzales. The United States government, hoping to protect the many American-owned companies in Mexico, backed one leader after another. American interference in the Revolution only added to the confusion and the violence.

Only through identifying with a leader could an average fighting man make sense out of this bizarre war. So instead of thinking of themselves as Democrats, Socialists, or monarchists, young men who fought for Villa became *Villistas* and those who fought for Carranza became *Carranzistas*.

Most common soldiers had no real idea of why they were

fighting. American journalist John Reed asked one young soldier what he was fighting for, and the man said, "Why, it is good, fighting; you don't have to work in the mines." A character in *The Underdogs,* a famous novel of the Revolution, says, "You will ask me why I stay on in the Revolution? The Revolution is a hurricane. The man who is swept up in it is no longer a man; he is a wretched dry leaf snatched away by the gale."

During ten years of unrelenting warfare, all sides committed outrageous atrocities. Railroads, towns, and estates were attacked and prisoners were shot or tortured.

EMILIANO ZAPATA

Somehow, above this sea of hatred and bloodshed, one leader rose like a new star in the heavens. To the south, the Indian Emiliano Zapata never forgot the reasons why he fought. His slogan was simply *Libertad y Tierra* (Liberty and Land). Zapata had grown up in plantation country where fellow Indians worked like slaves for wealthy landowners. He demanded that the plantations be broken up and each one of his soldiers be given a small farm. Mistrusting the revolutionary politicians, he took over the plantations, divided them among his men, and ordered the men to begin farming. Often Zapata's soldiers plowed fields while carrying rifles slung over their shoulders.

Zapata commanded fanatical loyalty from his white-clad farmer-warriors. They would have thrown themselves in front of blazing machine guns if Zapata had ordered it. Zapata's talks to his men were highlighted by simple, yet stirring, phrases: "Land and liberty is our only goal." "Men of the south, it is better to die on your feet than to live on your knees."

Revolutionary hero Emiliano Zapata (left) commanded fanatic loyalty from his followers in the southern state of Morelos.

Zapata's political enemies made countless attempts to kill him. But in the southern state of Morelos, he was invincible. Zapata was perhaps the best horseman in Mexico, and he knew every remote hideout in the rugged mountain country. And any peasant in the south would gladly have given his life to protect him. But in 1919, Zapata was lured into a trap set by a colonel named Guajardo and was shot by dozens of riflemen. His body was tied up in a nearby town square to prove to any upstart farmer that their hero was dead.

Yet even today, some people believe Zapata escaped death. They expect the Indian leader to ride out of the mountains once again to come to the aid of the peasants. A visitor in the hill country to the south can hear it in the whispers of the old people: "Yes, I saw him last night. I saw Emiliano. He was riding alone."

Chapter 5

TIES TO THE LAND

Through the ages, land has been sacred to the Mexican. When an Aztec prayed to his gods, he often began his prayers by kissing the earth. In Mexican history, the word *tierra* (land) has inspired hundreds of battle cries. Land was the major reason for the awesome bloodbath of 1910-20.

LANDOWNERSHIP

Landownership is still the single most explosive issue in Mexico. Out of the Revolution of 1910-20 came a new constitution with a very important land-reform clause. The purpose of the clause (Article 27) was to break up the old large estates and distribute the land to peasants. Postrevolutionary presidents tried to prove they were on the side of the poor by competing with each other to see who could redistribute the most land. Álvaro Obregón, who became president in 1920, gave away 3 million acres (1.2 million hectares). Plutarco Elías Calles, who followed him, redistributed 8 million acres (3.2 million hectares). The champion of the poor farmer was President Lázaro Cárdenas, who gave away 45 million acres (18.2 million hectares) during the

1930s. In all, some 130 million acres (52.6 million hectares) of land were given to poor farmers under the provisions of Article 27.

In spite of the land-reform law, many aristocratic landowners, especially those who were politicians, kept their old estates. The law states that a family may own no more than 100 hectares (247 acres) of irrigated land and 200 hectares (494 acres) of nonirrigated land. However, that law contains many loopholes, and a number of Mexicans continue to own farms and ranches that spread over thousands of acres. Today scarcely a month passes without a newspaper report telling of a band of angry farmers who have forced their way onto a large estate demanding that the land be redistributed.

Land is such a burning issue that even the smallest farmers fight over it. In remote areas, farms are often separated by boundary stones called *mojoneras.* If a mojonera should mysteriously shift during the night, a shooting war between farms can break out. Settling land disputes is the primary task of rural judges and peace officers. Neighboring villages that had land squabbles in the distant past carry grudges that can last a century.

A peculiarly Mexican system of landownership is called the *ejido.* Owning land under the ejido system goes back to the Indian era. An ejido is a collective farm controlled by all the people of a village. In one type of ejido, a family is given a five- to ten-acre (two- to four-hectare) plot to work. The family has the right to use the crops it grows in any way it wishes, but has no right to sell the land. On another type of ejido, everyone in a village works a large tract of land and shares the profits at harvesttime.

The president introduced land reforms with amendments to the constitution in 1991. These reforms included the abandonment of

These farmers near Oaxaca are using old-fashioned methods to harvest corn.

the collective farm system and allowing collective farmers to own, rent, or sell off their land. These measures are meant to increase productivity and private ownership.

LIFE ON THE FARMS

Scarcity of good farmland is one of the reasons why land-ownership is such an emotional issue. Most Mexican farmland is what agricultural experts call "marginal." It is rocky, poor in nutrients, and starved for rainfall. Only a few farms are blessed with rich topsoil and available water for irrigation.

The majority of Mexican farmers, especially those who work ejidos, are poor. Their homes are built of adobe brick, and are about the size of an American two-car garage. Most farmhouses have one or two windowless rooms where children, parents, and grandparents live together. Lacking beds, the family members sleep on straw mats call *petates*. They are spread over a hard-

Even the poorest Mexican farmhouses are usually brightened by splashes of color from flowerpots or gardens (left). Tortillas made the old-fashioned way, with a metate *and a* mano, *have a "taste of stone."*

packed dirt floor. Remote farm villages have no electricity and no reliable source of drinking water. Typically Mexican, however, is a well-tended flower garden that brightens even the poorest house.

Despite the hardships, Mexican farmers maintain their pride and dignity. Rarely will a farmer say he is poor. Instead, farm people with little money claim they are *humilde* (humble).

A farm family usually wakes up with the sun. Immediately upon rising, the women of the household begin toasting tortillas. Tortillas are flat, round cornmeal cakes that serve as the bread of Mexico. City people buy machine-made tortillas. In the poor farming communities, however, tortillas are made the old-fashioned way. Corn kernels are placed on a flat rock called a *metate* and crushed with a cylindrical-shaped roller called a *mano.* The cornmeal is then shaped into pancakelike patties and heated. Mexicans claim that tortillas made this way are superior to machine-made tortillas because the metate and mano give them a "taste of stone."

After a breakfast of tortillas and beans, the adults journey to the fields and the children go to school. In the last twenty years, the government has made a concerted effort to provide schools for all rural children. Still, many farm children go to school for only a few years, and a few never see the inside of a classroom.

Corn is the most widely grown crop in Mexico. For most farmers, a successful corn crop depends almost entirely on rainfall. Over the Central Plateau, the rainy season usually starts in late May and ends in September. For the farmer, the result of a year's work is determined by the rainfall during those four months. It is no wonder that religion has dominated the Mexican farmer's thinking for centuries.

If the rains have not fallen by June, the farm community will parade out statues of saints and plead with them to produce showers. If the rainless spell lasts until July, farmers can be seen shaking the statues as if to threaten the saints to make them bring rain. A few of the elderly farmers even turn their prayers to Tláloc, the ancient god of rain. If by September there is still no rain, the farm families try to determine what great sin they have committed to warrant this punishment.

For almost eight thousand years, corn, or maize, has fed the people of Mexico. At one time it was believed that knowledge of maize growing came from the gods. But maize, a gift from the gods, is often a curse for the farmer.

Before World War II, the great majority of Mexicans lived on

Government buildings and the town's main church border the traditional central plaza of León, with its bandstand, benches, and manicured trees.

farms. Today only 25 percent of the population lives in rural areas. The others live in cities or villages of five thousand people or more.

VILLAGE LIFE

Dotting the Mexican countryside are countless small villages. Many are mere clusters of farmhouses. Poor villages are drab and dusty, but some are tiny gems of postcard-perfect colonial architecture. Whether the villages are commonplace or attractive, they invariably have two things in common—a central plaza and a marketplace.

The Liberty Market in Guadalajara is housed in a large, warehouse-type building.

The village central plaza is a tradition the Spaniards established when they began founding towns in the New World. The plaza is a tree-shaded mini-park that is paved with flagstones and lined with park benches. It is also the heart of the village. The city hall and the biggest church can usually be found there.

In most villages, the marketplace is about a five-minute walk from the plaza. The central plaza is a Spanish tradition, but the marketplace is an Indian one.

Even the tiniest village has a marketplace. It is often housed in a large building that resembles a warehouse. Inside are small stands, each operated by one person, most often a woman. The stands are piled high with fresh fruits and vegetables—juicy pineapples, sweet mangoes, plump watermelons, tomatoes, and heads of lettuce. Along the walls of the building are refrigerated stands that hold meat and dairy products.

This street vendor is selling such staples of Mexican cuisine as tomatoes, chiles, onions, limes, and garlic.

Outside the market building, vendors spread sheets on the street and offer goods for sale. Many sellers make little pyramids of oranges and tomatoes and sell them by the *pila* (pile). Wall paintings drawn by artists more than a thousand years ago show Indian market vendors selling their fruits and vegetables in exactly the same fashion.

The market is open every day, but it is busiest during the once-a-week market days. On market days, farm families from miles around flock to the nearest village. Market activity spills into the streets as vendors set up stands near the market building. Some sellers have traveled many miles to city factories to buy goods the villagers rarely see, such as battery-operated toys and digital watches.

Rarely does a buyer accept the first price offered by a seller. Bargaining is a required practice. Mexicans often talk with their

*Among the various goods for sale in Mexican markets are American
T-shirts (left) and herbs for a great variety of disorders (right).*

hands. So a lively interchange between buyer and seller is both a
loud and an animated experience. Mexican housewives often
boast of their skill at bargaining in the market.

Some vendors sell cheap clothes that have been shipped all the
way from the United States. Even in the most remote mountain
villages, vendors sell T-shirts with lettering that proudly
announces "I Love New York," or "Bought at the Great Missouri
State Fair, 1982," or "I Survived the Chicago Blizzard of 1979."

One man sells strange-looking roots and dried leaves that he
keeps in glass jars. He is a *yerbero*—a seller of herbs. He claims the
herbs will cure a host of disorders. Above each jar he has placed a
sign: "To Cure Nervousness," "To Quit Smoking," or "For High
Blood Pressure." People buy the herbs, brew them into a tea, and
drink the tea hoping the curative powers will do their job.

Market day is also a weekly excuse for friends and relatives to get together to exchange greetings and gossip. When the market closes in the evening, the people gather in the central plaza. Often a band will play at a small bandstand in the center. While chatting and listening to music, the people walk in endless rings round and round the plaza. These evening strolls are an old Mexican custom called the *paseo.*

The paseo offers a perfect opportunity for boys and girls to flirt. According to the age-old "rules" of the paseo, the girls walk in a clockwise direction while the boys walk counterclockwise. Now and then they giggle at each other. If a boy wants to get to know a girl better, he will ask if he can walk with her. Walking together during the paseo can lead to dating. Walking together hand in hand during the paseo is the couple's way of telling the village they are sweethearts.

The paseo used to be practiced throughout Mexico. But for the most part, the custom has died out in the cities. Mexican cities are noisy, hurried places where people do not have the time for simple pleasures like the paseo.

LIFE IN THE CITIES

In Mexico there is a profound difference between city life and life on the farms or in the villages. In the rural areas, many customs have not changed in a hundred years. However, life in the cities has changed with the times and is now very much like city life in the United States or Canada. The status of women is a perfect example of the different customs in the cities. A farm woman usually marries young and then devotes her life to her home and her children, as did her mother and grandmother

The focal point of the city of Guanajuato is this bright yellow church, the Little Basilica, which was built in the seventeenth century.

Most rural Mexicans who go to Mexico City to look for work are forced to live in makeshift dwellings in the slum areas surrounding the city.

before her. In the cities, a young woman has far more opportunities. Schooling is more readily available, and she might have a chance of finding an interesting job.

Mexican country people move to the cities by the thousands, dreaming of greater opportunities. It is estimated that five thousand newcomers enter Mexico City each day looking for work. The new arrivals' dreams are very often shattered in the urban slums. Mexican slum dwellers live in shacks and lean-tos on the outskirts of the cities. The slums surrounding Mexico City cover hundreds of acres. The huge city airport lies in the middle of a teeming slum. Just across the street from the airport parking lot, thousands of people live in poverty. It is a section of Mexico City that few tourists ever visit.

Over fifty Mexican cities have more than 100,000 people. Five of the largest are Mexico City, Guadalajara, Netzahualcóyotl, Monterrey, and Puebla. Despite the slums, the streets are generally safer than many streets in United States cities, and Mexican cities are always exciting places to visit.

Guadalajara is a beautiful city of parks and broad boulevards.

Guadalajara is one of the most beautiful and exciting cities anywhere in the world. Its broad boulevards lined with palm trees lead to parks, fountains, and splendid old churches. Over the years, Guadalajara's stunning beauty has inspired artists and poets. The internationally famous painter José Orozco lived and worked there.

Because of its popularity as a tourist center, Acapulco is one of Mexico's most visited cities. Lying in the tierras calientes, the city has temperatures that rarely drop below 75 degrees Fahrenheit (23.9 degrees Celsius). Its silvery beaches and pounding surf attract vacationers from all over the world.

75

The lovely Spanish colonial town of Taxco is famous for its silver products.

The delightful city of Merida lies in the Yucatán Peninsula. The city attracts many visitors interested in Maya civilization. It is a starting-off place for a trip to the ruins of Chichen Itzá, an ancient Maya city. In Merida itself, there is a museum full of both ancient and contemporary Maya artwork. In 1524, the Spaniards founded Merida on the site of an ancient Maya city. Today it is a city of colonial structures and charming narrow streets. Windmills whirling on the city's rooftops are used to pump water from deep underground wells.

Another lovely city is Taxco, which lies some 70 miles (112.6 kilometers) southwest of Mexico City. Taxco is famous for its beautiful churches, its cobblestone streets, and its colonial houses with red tile roofs. The city was founded in 1529 by the original conquistador, Hernando Cortés. Over the years it has become internationally known for its silver products. Mexico's most talented silversmiths come to Taxco to develop their skills. They often work on shop benches open to the street so visitors can watch them fashion silver into delicate jewelry boxes, drinking goblets, candlestick holders, and many other objects.

The city of Monterrey lies far to the north, only 140 miles (225 kilometers) from Laredo, Texas. it is not a tourist attraction, but with a population of 1,069,238 it is Mexico's third largest city. It is also the country's leading center of industry. The city has sprawling iron and steel foundries. Its more than five hundred factories produce plastics, cement, automotive parts, textiles, and glassware. Most of Mexico's beer is brewed there. Despite its industry, unemployment is a major problem in Monterrey. Every day workers who are desperate for jobs flock to the city. Because there are not enough jobs to accommodate all these newcomers, shantytowns and teeming slums ring the outskirts of Monterrey.

El Paseo de la Reforma (left) is Mexico City's main boulevard. The Tower of Latin America (right) rises above the other buildings in the area.

MEXICO CITY

The king of all Mexican cities is its sprawling, bustling capital. The island city built by the Aztec is now a booming metropolis of more than fifteen million people, making it the sixth largest city in the world. The waters of old Lake Texcóco were drained long ago. Now the city suffers a chronic water shortage.

In the heart of Mexico City is a plaza called the *Zócalo*. In ancient times it was the site of a giant pyramid. The view from that plaza illustrates one of the most pressing problems facing Mexico City. For centuries, strollers near the plaza could see two

The lights of the Monument to the Revolution shimmer through Mexico City's evening smog (left). Most of the city's pollution comes from its huge number of motor vehicles (right).

lofty snowcapped volcanoes whose tips seemed to touch the sky. Today, however, few Mexico City residents under the age of twenty have seen those two volcanoes. They are hidden by a permanent cloud of smog that hangs over the capital. Mexico City has perhaps the worst air pollution of any large city in the world.

The mountains that form the Valley of Mexico give the capital bowl-shaped walls on three sides. With no place to escape, dirty air piles up over the city plaguing everyone with scratchy throats and burning eyes. Windows are kept closed even during summer heat. If left open overnight, a layer of grime covers furniture in the morning. It has been reported that nearly half the newborns in one of the city's major hospitals have enough lead in their blood to cause permanent physical and mental problems. As respiratory problems increase, schools and industries close on the worst days.

Most of Mexico City's pollution is caused by the millions of cars, trucks, and buses that crowd the streets, pouring pollutants into the air. Government regulations on vehicles have been lax. Air is relatively cleaner on weekends when motorists flee to the country.

An Indian vendor sells fruits and nuts outside a Mexico City metro station (left).
While digging the subway tunnel, workers found the ruins of an Aztec temple
buried below the streets (right) and built the Pino Suarez station around it.

But while pollution and nightmarish traffic reign above, below the streets purrs a modern miracle. In the early 1960s, Mexico City began constructing a magnificent subway system called the metro. Trains on the metro run quietly and swiftly. The 1983 price per ride was less than one penny. No ugly scribbling mars the walls. Instead, station walls are decorated with statues and paintings. The Pino Suarez station near the Zócalo is actually a mini-museum. While digging the subway tunnel, workers stumbled on the ruins of an Aztec temple. Rather than remove the temple, engineers built a station around it. So now riders can gaze at a centuries-old temple while waiting for their trains.

City planners hope that the metro will reduce automobile traffic and pollution. But there are new problems. The severe earthquakes of 1985 destroyed some of Mexico City's most important buildings. Many still have to be rebuilt, a difficult task for a relatively poor nation.

Chapter 6

MEXICANS AT EASE

Whether they live on farms, in villages, or in cities, Mexicans are among the hardest working people on earth. They bring to their work a driving energy that astounds foreign observers. But Mexicans enjoy their leisure time, too. Like people from other lands, they spend their free hours playing or watching sports, enjoying the arts, and giving parties.

SPORTS

Easily the most popular sport in Mexico is soccer. The country has a professional soccer league in which dozens of teams compete. Fans flock to the stadiums to cheer their favorite teams, or they crowd around television sets to watch the games.

The greatest international spectacle in soccer is the World Cup Games played once every four years. Mexico entered the 1978 World Cup with a fine team, and some soccer experts gave it an outside chance to win the championship. During the opening games, a strange hush fell over the country as nearly every man, woman, and child was glued to a television set. For the first time in anyone's memory, a visitor could not even get a shoeshine in

Mexico City. But the Mexican team lost an early-round game to Tunisia, and was quickly eliminated. A feeling of gloom hung over the country for weeks.

Baseball is the second most popular sport in Mexico. The Mexican baseball league attracts almost as many fans as does the soccer league. Baseball came to Mexico from the United States, but Mexico has returned the favor by providing the United States major leagues with some outstanding ball players. The first great Mexican player to journey north was Bobby Avila, who starred with the Cleveland Indians in the 1950s. His baseball fame made Avila a hero in Mexico. He was later elected governor of his home state of Veracruz. More recently, a nineteen-year-old Mexican named Fernando Valenzuela joined the Los Angeles Dodgers. He threw a dazzling screwball that sportswriters later called "Fernando's Fadeaway." The pitch won Valenzuela both the Rookie of the Year and the Cy Young awards in 1981.

Mexicans excel in many other sports as well. Their tennis players have long been strong in world competition. In the Olympics, Mexicans have dominated in race walking. Members of the Tarahumara Indian tribe in northern Mexico are known for their incredible endurance as long-distance runners. Their tribal races sometimes stretch over 200 miles (322 kilometers).

A game unique to Mexico is called *fronton*. It is played with tennis rackets and a tennis ball, and involves bouncing the ball off a wall. The game of *jai alai* is also played against a wall, and is possibly the fastest game in the world. Using wicker scoops called *cestas*, players fire a ball against the wall as though it were shot from a rifle. A successful jai alai player must have catlike reflexes.

The Spaniards brought bullfighting to Mexico, and it remains a popular attraction. Also popular are the special Mexican rodeos

Mexican rodeos called charriadas *(left) and bullfights (right) are popular attractions.*

called *charriadas.* American rodeo performers marvel at the skills
displayed by Mexican horsemen called *charros.*

MUSIC

Mexicans can find any kind of music they prefer. For lovers of
classical music, Mexico has at least eight symphony orchestras and
more than five choruses. For rock fans, some blaring band can be
found in every good-sized village, and dozens are in the cities.

The curious visitor can also discover the thrill of traditional
Mexican music. This may come from a strolling group of
troubadours called *mariachis,* or from two or three singing
cowboys called *nortenos.* Whatever its source, there is a quality to
the music that non-Mexicans can only imitate, never duplicate.

A mariachi *band entertains guests on a flower-trimmed boat at the floating gardens of Xochimilco, near Mexico City.*

It is said that French soldiers helped create the famous Mexican mariachi bands. During their brief occupation of Mexico, many French soldiers married Mexican girls. For their wedding services, the Frenchmen hired small bands to entertain the guests. The bands began to be called mariachis after the French word for marriage.

The typical mariachi group has six to eight players—a singer-leader, two violin players, two horn players, two guitarists, and a bass player. The members dress in uniforms decorated with sparkling silver sequins and wear broad-brimmed hats. They wander about plazas and in and out of restaurants and taverns. For a fee, they play any song a customer wishes to hear. The customer often sings along or cries out the shrill "Ay-ay-ays" whenever the band hits a mournful note. Mariachi music is heard throughout the world, and has come to symbolize Mexico.

Norteno music is little known outside of Mexico, but is wildly popular within the country. It is sometimes called *ranchero* music because it is sung by ranch hands. It has been compared to American country and western music.

A norteno group usually has three players—one plays an accordion, another a guitar, and a singer-leader plays a piece of wood. That's right, the leader's instrument is a piece of wood. Wired to his belt is a foot-long piece of two-by-four. The leader sings and raps on the piece of wood with two drumsticks. Norteno custom demands that the leader show the emotion of the song. If the song is sad, tears slip down his face. If it is lively, he leaps high in the air and clicks his heels while wildly beating on the two-by-four.

Mexicans have sung folk songs for hundreds of years. The famous folk song "La Cucaracha" ("The Cockroach") was sung by the soldiers who fought for Pancho Villa during the 1910-20 Revolution. The song has dozens of verses. In one verse Villa's soldiers poke fun at their overweight leader:

Una cosa me da risa	One thing makes me laugh
Pancho Villa sin camisa	Pancho Villa without his shirt

THE MOVIES

The broad boulevards of Mexico City are lined with movie houses, and they are usually jammed with fans. Since Mexican history is so rich in drama, Mexican filmmakers favor historical subjects. Two historical films shot in the 1970s were *Aquellos Años* (*Those Years*), a film about the tragic story of Maximilian and Carlota, and *Zapata*, a biographical film telling the life story of the hero Emiliano Zapata. Both were sprawling historical epics, beautifully photographed. A touching 1950 film called *Los Olvidados* (The Forgotten Ones) told the story of an adolescent farm boy lost on the streets of Mexico City. It won international acclaim.

Foreign movies, especially those from the United States, are also popular in Mexico. By law, no "dubbing" of Spanish voices for foreign voices is allowed. Instead, the translation is done entirely with printed Spanish subtitles flashed on the bottom of the screen. The law was passed in the 1950s for a very practical reason. At that time, many Mexicans did not know how to read, and the government hoped to encourage literacy. Since dubbed Spanish was forbidden, illiterate moviegoers had to learn how to read if they hoped to understand foreign movies.

Of all types of Hollywood movies, westerns have been most popular in Mexico over the years. Perhaps that is because the history of the American frontier and Mexican history are so closely intertwined.

THE ARTS

Mexico is a land of dazzling colors. From flowers and the bright sky, colors seem to gush forth. It is no wonder that for centuries this flood of colors has inspired artists to paint.

Mexicans are world famous for their wall paintings (murals). Ancient muralists were busy in Maya and Aztec times. Even today, fading murals still decorate the ruins of temples. In the modern era, Mexican muralists reached their height during the 1910-20 Revolution. Three outstanding muralists of that era were José Orozco, Diego Rivera, and David Siqueiros. Because Mexican

These murals were painted by David Siqueiros (left) and Diego Rivera (right).

society was in such turmoil during the Revolution, many of their murals were deeply political. On the walls of the government headquarters building at the Zócalo in Mexico City spreads a series of murals painted by Diego Rivera. Each mural shows an episode in Mexican history. The final mural seems to predict that the Socialists will triumph in the country.

Modern Mexican painters are more personal than they are political. They prefer painting wild pictures of a village market at sunrise to representational scenes of a revolutionary battlefield. To modern Mexican painters, the revolution was an experience in history, and they feel no need to declare their patriotism through their art. "I am Mexican without difficulty and without worrying about it," says painter Juan Soriano. "For me the only important revolution is that of taste." Still, modern Mexican painters will always be compared to the masters who led the artistic explosion of the 1910-20 revolutionary period.

Architect Juan O'Gorman decorated the University of Mexico Library with a stone-tile mosaic of Indian scenes (left). In 1735, the facade of Sanborn's House of Tile, former home of a Spanish aristocrat, was covered with the famous blue Puebla tile (right).

The three eras of Mexican history can be seen most strikingly in the country's architecture. Religion dominated the buildings of the pre-Columbian Indians. Many of their huge, flat-topped stone temples still stand in clusters in the countryside. Spanish colonial architecture is seen more in the old sections of cities and in the historic towns. Sweeping, graceful arches highlight colonial buildings. Church architecture of the colonial period is particularly impressive. The massive National Cathedral in Mexico City, which was begun in 1573, is a fine example of colonial architecture. Much of modern Mexican architecture is functional glass and steel, and looks like modern architecture anywhere else in the world. But some of today's architects have attempted to combine Indian art with modern construction. Architect Juan O'Gorman created a fascinating library building for

Mexican folk artists produce an amazing variety of handicrafts including the Indian pottery, straw baskets, and colorful woven goods shown here.

the University of Mexico. Using stone tiles, he fashioned a mosaic of Indian scenes on the outside wall of the building. In all, some seven million stone chips were used to decorate the library's walls.

The folk art of Mexico is renowned throughout the world. Mexican silversmiths and jewelers fashion exquisite creations. Entire mountain villages are known for their production of certain handicrafts. One village produces the famous Mexican blue tiles, another is known for its straw baskets, and another for its blown-glass figurines.

MEXICAN FOOD

Americans have two long-standing misconceptions about Mexican food. First, they believe that all Mexican food is fiery hot. Wrong. For the most part, Mexican food is no more spicy than American food. But a Mexican meal, whether served at a

Chiles en nogadas *(left) is a famous holiday dish created to celebrate Mexican Independence Day. The green chiles, white cream, and red pomegranate seeds are the colors of the flag of Mexico. Some of the staples of the Mexican diet (right) are tomatoes, chiles, onions, a variety of peppers, and, in the center, the tiny green* tomatillos *used in the famous Mexican green sauce.*

restaurant or in a private home, comes with a side saucer of chili sauce. A person can spoon the sauce over his food to make it as spicy as he wishes. Another side dish frequently served with Mexican meals is whole chili peppers. Newcomers should beware of them because chili peppers can set your mouth on fire.

The second misconception about Mexican cuisine is created by the newer American restaurants advertising "Mexican food." Wrong. Most of those restaurants serve the kind of food that evolved among Mexican people living in Texas. The "Tex-Mex" dishes are usually delightful, but they are not genuinely Mexican. A story is told about an American tourist accustomed to Tex-Mex food who entered a Mexico City restaurant and ordered a bowl of chili. The waiter shrugged his shoulders and brought the tourist a bowl of jalapeño chili peppers. To the Mexican waiter this was chili. The popular American dish called chili con carne evolved in Texas, not Mexico.

The humble tortilla forms the basis of most Mexican dishes. Enchiladas and tacos are tortillas filled with meat, chicken, or cheese and then folded or rolled. Enchiladas are baked and usually covered with some kind of sauce. A particularly delicious sauce is called *mole*. It is chocolaty brown and rich to the taste. Cooks keep the recipe for their favorite mole sauce a secret and hand it down only to family members.

Nearly every Mexican meal is served with beans. Often the beans are mashed and served as *frijoles refritos* (refried beans). Rice, too, accompanies most meals. Mexicans eat a stack of tortillas at nearly every meal.

Mexicans prepare some sinfully delicious desserts. One is a custard pudding called *flan*. It is made of eggs, sugar, and milk and tastes heavenly to those who do not worry about gaining weight. Chocolate drinks are favored in Mexico. The Aztec so revered chocolate that they used chocolate beans for money. A nutritious fruit drink served in the markets is called a *liquado*. It is made by putting fruit such as half a banana, a few strawberries, and a slice of pineapple into a blender, then filling the blender with orange juice and liquefying the whole concoction. A liquado for breakfast is a marvelous way to start the day.

VIVA LA FIESTA

Good food and music are two of the ingredients that make up a party. Parties are called *fiestas*. A rollicking fiesta is an excuse for everyone to go just a little bit crazy.

Outsiders sometimes accuse Mexicans of hiding their true feelings. The stoic Mexican often gives the impression that he or she is as unmovable as the earth itself. No one, claim the outsiders, can be as inwardly calm as the faces most Mexicans show to the world. During fiestas, however, the Mexican character changes. It becomes one of wild and even alarming excitement.

Marigolds, the pre-Columbian flower of death, are always for sale in the markets on the Day of the Dead. Women decorate graves with flowers and long candles and keep an all-night vigil at the graves. At dawn, they are joined by the men for a day of picnicking and cleaning the cemetery.

The famous Mexican writer Octavio Paz says of his countrymen and their fiestas, "[Fiesta] night is when friends who have not exchanged more than the prescribed courtesies for months, drink together, trade confidences, weep over the same troubles, discover they are brothers, and sometimes to prove it, kill each other. The night is full of song and loud cries. The lover wakes up his sweetheart with an orchestra. . . . Nobody talks quietly. Hats fly in the air. Laughter and curses ring like silver pesos. . . . [The Mexican] seeks to escape from himself, to leap over the wall of solitude that confines him during the rest of the year. All are possessed by the violence and the frenzy. Their souls explode. . . . "

Mexicans are ingenious when thinking of reasons to hold a fiesta. Each profession has an annual "day" to celebrate its work. During a fiesta day honoring schoolteachers, every child in a class brings some sort of gift. Another fiesta day honors construction workers. The men go to their job sites, then sit down, listen to a hired band, and drink together. On the fiesta day celebrating postmen, each household on a route offers food and drink to the letter carrier. Even the dead have their fiesta day. The *Dia de los Muertos* (Day of the Dead) is not a sad affair. Rather it is a day to celebrate with the spirit of a dead friend or relative.

The whole country becomes involved in religious and patriotic

During the Christmas season, piñatas (left) are sold and pictures made from strands of electric lights are suspended above Mexico City streets (right).

fiestas. Countless different regional fiestas are celebrated by the people of certain towns and villages.

Religious fiestas are usually solemn occasions, but they arouse passionate feelings. The most important religious fiesta is Guadalupe Day, held on December 12. From all over the country, rich and poor alike journey to the chapel on the hill where it is said that the Virgin of Guadalupe appeared to the Indian peasant Juan Diego. Some people walk in shoes riddled with holes, while others ride in limousines. Many believe the Virgin will still perform miracles if only she is asked in the right way. So they bring her gifts along with their special prayers.

Christmas is a nine-day celebration. On the nine nights before Christmas, people act out the journey of Mary and Joseph to Bethlehem. The ceremonies performed each night are called *posadas*. After a posada, children are allowed the age-old pleasure of breaking the *piñata*. Piñatas are papier-mâché containers often shaped like animals, usually horses or dogs. Hidden inside are pieces of candy, toys, or other treasures. The piñata is hung from a hook. Blindfolded children break it with sticks and then scramble to pick up the treats.

Patriotic fiestas are often boisterous events. The two most important patriotic celebrations are *Cinco de Mayo* and Independence Day. Cinco de Mayo (the Fifth of May) honors the 1862 Battle of Puebla in which ragtag Mexican forces defeated an army of French professional soldiers. It is a day for a stirring speech by the president, and for a grand military parade down one of Mexico City's broad boulevards.

Mexican Independence Day falls on September 16. In the evening, people gather in the central plazas of towns and villages all over the republic to hear their mayors give what is called the *Grito de Dolores* (Cry of Dolores). A mayor usually starts his *grito* by shouting, "*Mejicanos, viva nuestros héroes*!" ("Mexicans, long live our heroes!") "Viva!" the crowd in the plaza shouts back. Then the mayor calls each hero by name. "Viva Hidalgo!" "Viva!" answers the crowd. "Viva Allende!" "Viva!" the crowd repeats. And finally the mayor cries out, "Viva Mexico!" At that moment, a band blares the Mexican national anthem, church bells peal, fireworks explode, and even foreign visitors become instant Mexicans as everyone roars into the night, "Viva Mexico! Viva Mexico! Viva Mexico!"

Regional fiestas are usually the wildest celebrations of the year. Each town or village honors some event with a one-day fiesta. Perhaps a century ago the town was in the grips of a bandit gang and was rescued by some local fearless hero. Once a year, that town will stage a reenactment of the climactic gunfight and then spend the rest of the evening holding a party on the plaza.

Regional fiestas are an excuse for the normally hardworking, calm, and uncomplaining Mexican to get just a little bit wild. A really amazing regional fiesta is held every September in a mountain town called San Miguel de Allende.

SAN MIGUEL DAY

The town of San Miguel de Allende is a treasure of Spanish colonial architecture. Its central plaza, lined with trees and park benches, stands in the shadow of a tall church. On a tower beside the church a huge clock chimes every fifteen minutes. The town's architecture is so classic that it is one of three villages in the nation that have been declared national monuments. By law, no old building can be torn down or a new building erected.

Normally, San Miguel is a quiet, sleepy place of about forty thousand people. Many Americans, Canadians, and Europeans live there because they enjoy the unhurried pace of life. But once a year the entire town goes mad.

San Miguel Day commemorates the feast day of St. Michael (Miguel), the patron saint of the town. Before the sun comes up, people crowd into the plaza as tightly as blades of grass on a lawn. It is said that every Mexican named Miguel must come to San Miguel for this fiesta. There are millions of Miguels in Mexico, so they could not all have come to the town. It only seems that way.

The people have gathered in the plaza to start the fiesta by "waking up" St. Michael. Breathlessly they wait for the giant clock to chime 4:00 A.M. At four the plaza explodes. A dozen different mariachi bands play a dozen different tunes all at once. Fireworks whiz and bang. Bells in every church tower in town peal wildly. The din is terrific. The people make an unearthly amount of noise. After all, they are trying to wake up St. Michael, and he has been dead for centuries.

Daring young men face the bulls during the Fiesta of San Miguel.

When the sun comes up, police clear the streets surrounding the plaza and put up steel barriers at the plaza's entrances. At about 10:00 A.M., a man opens the doors of a huge trailer-truck parked on the main street. Down a ramp thunder four or five giant black bulls. In the streets are a couple of hundred young men and a scattering of young women. They are demonstrating their bravery (or foolishness) by standing up to the bulls. They scatter like bowling pins when they see the bulls, heads down, charging at them. But a few young men hold capes and actually try to fight the bulls as if they were *matadors* in a ring. The unluckly ones are butted practically into the plaza. Is this dangerous? Of course, as bulls have killed some. But at fiesta time people laugh at danger.

When the bulls are finally exhausted, they are rounded up and herded back into the truck. Now a long parade snakes through the streets. It is led by the handsome horsemen called *charros* and their girl friends called *charras*. A float built on a truck shows St.

Colorfully costumed Conchero dancers perform during the fiesta (left), and in the evening fireworks called castillos *burst into brilliant colors (right).*

Michael fighting the eternal battle of good against evil. On the float, a child dressed as St. Michael holds a cardboard sword over his head and appears about to strike another child dressed as the devil. Also in the parade are Indian dancers who wear headdresses sporting feathers two feet long. On their ankles and wrists are bracelets with tiny jingling bells attached to them. The Indians break out of the parade, assemble in the churchyard, and begin a slow, circular dance. They will dance tirelessly throughout the day and into the night.

In the evening, workers erect tall poles with strings of fireworks covering them like spiders' webs. The poles look like castle spires so they are called *castillos* (castles). A man lights a fuse and the castillos burst into brilliant colors. Pinwheels attached to the castillos whirl, scream like ambulance sirens, and leave circles of fire burning in the night. The rockets that whoosh out of the castillos and explode in the dark sky look like a flock of flaming

When the mariachi bands have played their last lively note and the Indians (left)
have danced their last jingling step, the fiesta crowds leave the plaza and
once again San Miguel becomes a sleepy town with an unhurried pace of life (right).

butterflies. The people cheer and gasp oohs and aahs as the castillos work their magic.

Mariachi bands weave through the crowded plaza and stop to play whenever they find a customer. People sing and dance to the music. In the churchyard, the Indians continue their endless circular dance. The tiny bells on their ankles and wrists jingle with each step.

All evening the plaza hums with the fiesta. Finally, at about four A.M., the people begin to stream home. The fiesta has lasted twenty-four exhausting hours. After the streets are swept up, San Miguel de Allende again becomes a sleepy town with an unhurried pace of life. It will remain that way—at least for another year until the next San Miguel Day.

Chapter 7

CHALLENGES OF
MODERN MEXICO

Modern Mexico was born in the blood and fire of the Revolution of 1910-20. The conflict was so destructive that its memory has remained branded on the minds of Mexicans for generations. But out of the bloodshed came a political stability that has lasted until this day.

THE MEXICAN GOVERNMENT SINCE THE REVOLUTION

The most important document to be born during the Revolution was the constitution of 1917. It was the first constitution of any major country in the world to recognize the right of labor unions to organize. It also contained Article 27, which in principle limited the amount of land that one family could own.

From the chaos of the Revolution came a stable political party. Earlier Mexican political parties had been temporary combinations of various groups organized by a presidential candidate. The National Revolutionary party, formed in the 1920s, was a permanent institution that resembled the political parties of the United States. Now called the Institutional Revolutionary party (PRI), it usually wins every major election by huge majorities. However, in 1988 an opposition coalition, the National Democratic Front and an opposition party, the National Action party, won almost half the seats in the Chamber of Deputies. No longer could the president depend on a two-thirds vote of the Chamber required to amend the constitution.

The constitution provides for a government that functions under three branches: executive, legislative, and judicial. Since the 1910-20 war, however, the president of Mexico has had great power over Congress and the courts. Unlike the president of the United States, the Mexican president does not need the approval of Congress to make important decisions.

THE MEXICAN ECONOMY

The Mexican population is growing faster than that of almost any other country in the world. In 1900, the population of Mexico stood at 13.6 million people. There are now more than that many people living in the Mexico City area alone. The estimated population of Mexico in the year 2000 is 102,555,000. If this rate of increase continues, Mexico could double its population in twenty-six years. This skyrocketing population is the greatest influence on the Mexican economy.

About 55 percent of Mexican people are under the age of twenty. Every year, hundreds of thousands of new workers begin to seek jobs. Most have little luck. About half of the Mexican work force is unemployed or underemployed. Unable to find jobs, young workers survive by selling lottery tickets, shining shoes, or weaving in and out of big city traffic jams to peddle newspapers.

Left: The Legislative Palace in Mexico City, where Congress meets
Right: These women, among the millions of unemployed workers in Mexico, try to survive by weaving in and out of big city traffic jams to sell lottery tickets.

Mexico's marginal farmland cannot feed its burgeoning population, although agriculture has improved through use of more modern equipment and methods. Climate makes it necessary to purchase much food, even corn for tortillas, from other countries.

In 1994 the North American Free Trade Agreement (NAFTA) went into effect. This agreement between Mexico, Canada, and the United States should further boost the economy by increasing trade and eliminating tariffs between these countries.

To buy food, Mexico must have something to sell to foreign customers. Mexico is one of the largest oil producers in the world and some geologists believe undiscovered fields could make it as oil-rich as Saudi Arabia. However, oil production is not what economists call a "labor intensive industry." It does not create many jobs. Manufacturing is a labor intensive industry. During the 1970s, the Mexican government used money borrowed from foreign banks to encourage manufacturing and for large-scale government projects that it hoped would create much-needed jobs. The government believed it could pay back the loans with revenue from oil sales. But oil prices dropped in the early 1980s, and Mexico found itself $80 billion in debt and with less income to pay back its loans.

The enormous foreign debt triggered the worst financial crisis in Mexican history. The country was forced to borrow just to pay the interest on its many loans.

The debt led to a massive devaluation of the peso, the basic unit of currency. The peso went from 22.5 to the U.S. dollar in 1981 to 143 to the dollar in January, 1984. This devaluation brought devastating inflation. A hamburger that once cost ten pesos zoomed to one hundred pesos. A bunch of bananas that once cost two pesos suddenly jumped to twenty. Foreign goods disappeared from the stores because no one could afford them.

"Como se viven los pobres?" ("How do the poor people live?") is a bewildering question asked by better-off Mexicans coping with soaring prices. One way a poor person manages is by buying only government subsidized foods such as tortillas, beans, and rice. Subsidies make these basic foods affordable, but treats such as roast beef or ice cream are impossible.

By 1993 the government introduced a new peso or currency that would cut three zeros from the old peso, but both new and old pesos would continue to circulate with prices posted in both forms. This was done to simplify business transactions which often run into billions of old pesos. The government continues to sell state-owned businesses according to privatization plans, in efforts to reduce national debt and promote economic growth. Privatization has led to increased competitiveness and better services. Proceeds from sale of state holdings have been used for new social programs.

Maria's mother runs a small shop in downtown Mexico City, much like this one, that caters to American tourists.

THE GAP BETWEEN RICH AND POOR

Maria Valdez is thirteen and lives in a section of Mexico City called *Las Lomas de Chapultepec* (the Hills of Chapultepec). It is an area of sturdy single-family homes near Mexico City's famous Chapultepec Park. Maria's father is a dentist. Her mother runs a small shop downtown that caters to American tourists. Maria works part-time in the shop. She enjoys her work because it gives her a chance to practice English. English is her favorite subject at school. Maria attends a private school for which her parents pay about fifty dollars a month. Classroom size averages twenty students per teacher, and the teachers are all experienced professionals.

In Maria's house there is a color television, a stereo, and a piano. The Valdez family also owns a car and uses it to escape

This elegant home is in Las Lomas de Chapultepec, *where Maria Valdez lives.*

Mexico City's smog for weekends in the country. When Maria was a little girl, her family visited her uncle in the United States. Maria still has exciting memories of her one and only trip to *Disneylandia*. But that was before the crash of the peso. Now her father grumbles that the only Mexicans who can travel abroad are the superrich or the illegal workers. Luckily, the Valdez family purchased most of their appliances before the devaluation of the peso. The peso price of their Japanese-made color television set tripled in 1983.

Maria's family has both a maid and a gardener. All of her neighbors have servants, too. Domestic help is still cheap for well-to-do Mexicans. Both of Maria's parents come from prominent Mexico City families. Her oldest brother is now attending medical school. Despite the collapse of the peso and subsequent government controls, Maria's family and her neighbors continue to prosper. At parties in Las Lomas de Chapultepec, the adults have a favorite toast. They clink their glasses and say, "To Mexico. Still the greatest country in the world to be rich in."

This is a typical home in Netzahualcoyotl, where Juan Rivera lives.

About a forty-five minute subway ride from Maria's house is a suburb with the difficult-to-pronounce Aztec name Netzahualcoyotl. Before World War II, the area was a barren, rocky wasteland that supported only a few cactus plants. Today it has a population of more than a million. One of the people living there is twelve-year-old Juan Rivera.

Juan, his mother and father, and four brothers and sisters live in a house that has grown over the years. It started out as a one-room adobe brick home that measured about 20 feet by 20 feet (6 meters by 6 meters). The family has since built an additional room of wooden stakes and corrugated aluminum. Many of Juan's neighbors live in houses constructed entirely of scrap lumber, packing boxes, and corrugated aluminum. Despite being in the middle of a dismal slum, Juan's mother keeps her house remarkably clean. The outside walls are lined with shelves holding potted plants and flowers.

These village schoolchildren are marching back to class after recess.

Juan attends school, but wants to drop out to look for a job. Both his parents insist that he stay in school. At Juan's school, the children sit two to a desk and share textbooks. There are sixty students in his classroom. Juan's teacher is a nineteen-year-old girl who just finished normal school (teacher's college). As she gains more experience, the teacher will probably move on to a private school where the working conditions are far better.

Juan's family came to the Mexico City area ten years ago from an ejido farm in the state of Guanajuato. Nearly every resident of Netzahualcoyotl is a recent immigrant from the country. Juan's father works as a helper on a truck that delivers soft drinks to stores. He is paid by the driver at the end of the day. Often the driver decides he needs no help. Then Juan's father earns no wages. Juan's mother embroiders potholders which she tries to sell at the market. Juan sells newspapers. Sometimes he wanders the streets with an armload of papers until ten or eleven at night. The Rivera family has a used gas stove but no refrigerator. At one time, they owned an old black-and-white television set but had to sell it for food money. The family eats mainly tortillas, beans, and rice. Chicken on a Sunday is a very special treat.

About once a year, the Rivera family scrapes together enough money to take a bus to their old village in the country. There Juan,

To close the gap between rich and poor, Mexico must provide jobs for its millions of unemployed workers, such as these electricians, plumbers, and masons who are waiting outside the fence of the National Cathedral hoping for job offers.

despite his poverty, feels he is rich. Juan's country cousins live in homes with dirt floors. They have to walk half a mile to get a bucket of water. There is no electricity. But the air is clean, and Juan can dash about as he pleases without worrying about the speeding cars and trucks he continually has to dodge in Mexico City. On one visit to the country, Juan began teaching one of his cousins to read. He is Juan's age, but has never gone to school.

Juan Rivera lives only a few miles from Maria Valdez, but their life-styles are worlds apart. In the past, the distance between the rich and poor had led to revolution and civil war. Even in 1994 rebels such as the Zapatista National Liberation Army (EZLN) launched uprisings in impoverished states in order to gain international recognition and negotiate government reforms that would upgrade living standards of the Indians. Reforms would include housing, electricity, clinics, education, redistribution of land, and democratic elections without fraud. For many workers one hope is still to sneak across the border into the United States.

THE PLIGHT OF THE ILLEGAL WORKERS

An estimated two to three million Mexican illegals live in the United States. For decades, Mexican workers have slipped across the border *"bajo alambre"* (underneath the barbed wire), as their saying goes. In recent years, the stream of illegals has become a flood. In 1960, United States immigration authorities arrested 22,687 Mexican illegals. In 1978, that number had leaped to almost a million.

Those arrested are usually put on buses and sent back to Mexico. Once on Mexican soil, most immediately plot a course to return to the United States. In the 1990s Mexico and the United States formed an integrated border plan of cooperation between the two countries to further resolve the problem of illegal entries into the United States.

American employers know that Mexicans work hard. They will also accept low-paying jobs that American workers are likely to turn down. Many illegal workers give up on applying for legal immigration or work permits in the United States because only a comparative few are accepted each year.

Studies show that the typical illegal worker is a man with a family back in Mexico. His needs are simple, so if he can find work, even at the minimum wage, he can mail back enough money to support his wife and children. One such illegal worker is Ramiro Tovar, a father of three, who first sneaked across the border seeking work in 1960.

"I didn't have any choice," Tovar told an American writer

during a 1980 interview. "I had to look for a better way of life." Tovar grew up on a tiny farm in the state of Zacatecas. "Maybe we would have a little corn and some beans," he said. "But we were always dependent on rain to have enough to eat."

Hoping that his children would have a better way of life, Tovar saved up twenty-five dollars and paid it to a "coyote." A coyote is a secret guide whose business is smuggling aliens across the border. Today, coyotes charge an illegal worker hundreds of dollars. Tovar found a job on a Nevada cattle ranch that paid two hundred dollars a month. For Tovar in 1960, that was a fortune, and it was the beginning of a new era in his life. "I was a real wetback," he said.

Over the next twenty years, Tovar lost count of how many times he returned to Mexico to visit his family and then crept back across the border to seek work. Twelve times he was caught and sent back to Mexico, only to turn about immediately and head for the border. While in the United States, Tovar held a steady job.

Like most other illegal workers, Tovar would be happy to stay at home, but he views Mexico as a land with little opportunity. "I know how it feels to suffer, but the only way to better yourself is to come [to the United States] illegally. In Mexico there is inspiration but no hope."

THE INDESTRUCTIBLE MEXICAN SPIRIT

According to some experts, the future of Mexico is still gloomy. The country owes billions of dollars. Almost half its workers have no jobs. But government reforms and privatization of most business have resulted in a much more diversified economy and reduction of inflation from 159 percent in 1987 to about 10 percent by 1994.

Political banners like these were much in evidence during the campaign of Miguel de la Madrid, who was elected president in 1982.

In 1982 Miguel de la Madrid took office as president. He launched programs designed to reduce Mexico's debt, reduce government waste, and improve education.

In 1988 Carlos Salinas de Gortari became president. He continued the reforms, broadening their scope. By the 1990s he introduced educational reforms that resulted in churches having control over religious studies and states controlling local schools. However, protests against government continued, with accusations of election fraud. In 1994, with results indicating necessity of shared power, Ernesto Zedillo Ponce de León was elected president.

Efforts of individual Mexicans are important in improving their society. Mexican spirit is indestructible. The people make the country unconquerable with belief in simple virtues—loyalty to family, faith in God, and hard work. They endure suffering without complaint, and are able to laugh at their troubles.

Finally, Mexicans possess a sense of kindness that is almost unheard-of in the modern world. This sense of kindness was witnessed by an American late one night in Mexico City.

A woman led three small children into a restaurant where the American sat alone at a table. The woman wore clothes from the best shops. The children, although dressed in their Sunday best, wore clothes bought at the cheapest stand in a village market. Mexicans readily observe the appearance of their countrymen, and the waiter and the owner of the restaurant were quick to notice that the woman had light skin, while the children looked to be Indian. Also, the children were handicapped. The two girls (who were five or six) were blind, and the boy (about nine) had a clubfoot.

The restaurant had few customers, and the waiter took the woman's order at once. While they were eating, it seemed clear that the children were puzzled by the knives and forks. In their country homes, people eat with tortillas—scooping the food off their plates with a tortilla, then eating the food, tortilla and all. The waiter, himself mostly Indian, noticed the children's difficulty. Without waiting to be asked, he brought an extra basket of tortillas. As he placed the basket on the table, he smiled knowingly at the woman.

The owner of the restaurant had been watching, too. Like the woman, he had light skin, indicating a Spanish heritage and perhaps old money wealth. He whispered to the waiter that the woman was probably on some mission with the children. Perhaps she was bringing them to a Mexico City doctor. The American, who had lived in Mexico for many years, overheard his words. He also heard the owner tell the waiter to take a slice of cake to each child. The women thanked the waiter and asked for her check. The owner shook his head and smiled. "You are doing a good deed," he said. "Now let me do one, too. The dinner is my gift."

The American watched this simple but moving scene. He tried to remember the last time he had seen such an act of quiet kindness in his own country. The American paid his bill, stepped outside, and whispered into the night, "Viva Mexico. Viva Mexico."

MAP KEY

Acambaro	C4, m13
Acaponeta	C3
Acapulco	D5
Acatlan	D5
Acayucan	D5, n14
Agua Prieta	B4
Aguascalientes, Ciudad	C4, m12
Aguascalientes (AGS), state	C4, k12
Ahualulco de Mercado	m12
Alamo	m15
Altamirano, Ciudad	B4
Alvarado	D5
Amacuzac, river	n, o14
Ameca	C4, m11
Ameca, river	m11
Apam	n12
Apatzingan	n12
Apizaco	n14
Aquiles Serdan	B3
Aranchas	m12
Armeria, river	n12
Arriaga	D6
Atotonilco el Alto	g9
Atotonilco de Zaragoza	m12
Atoyac, river	n14
Autlan de Navarro	D4, n11
Ayutla	h9, n14
Azcapotzalco	A3
Bacerac	D7
Bahía Chetumal, bay	B2
Bahía de Ballenas, bay	C2, 3
Bahía de Banderas, bay	C2, 3
Bahía de la Paz, bay	C2
Bahía Sebastián Vizcaíno, bay	B2
Baja California, state	C3, m11
Baja California Norte, terr.	A1, 2; B1, 2
Baja California Sur, terr.	B2, 3; C2, 3
Balsas, river	D4, n13
Bay of Campeche	C5, 6; D5, 6
Blanco, river	n15
Bolaños, river	m11, 12
Cabo Catoche, cape	C7
Cabo Colnett, cape	A1
Cabo Corrientes, cape	C3, m11
Cabo Falso, cape	C3
Cabo Lobos, cape	B2
Cabo Rojo, cape	B2
Cabo San Lucas, cape	C2, 3
Cabo San Lucas, city	C2, 3
Cabo Tepoca, cape	A2
Caborca	A2
Camacho	C4
Camargo, Ciudad	B4
Campeche, city	C6
Campeche, state	C6
Canal de Chalco	D6, h9
Canal de Garay	h9
Cananea	A2
Cárdenas	D6, k14
Carmen, Ciudad del	C7
Carmen, island	B2
Cerritos	C4
Ceylaya	m13
Chapala	m12
Charcas	C4
Chetumal, Ciudad	D7
Chiapa de Corzo	D6, E6
Chiapas, state	D6
Chichen Itza	C7
Chico, river	n13
Chihuahua, city	D4, n12
Chihuahua, state	B3, 4
Chilpancingo	D5, o14
Chimalhuacán	D5
Choix	n14
Coahuila, state	B3
Coatepec	B4, C4
Coatzacoalcos	D6
Cocula	m12
Colima, city	C4, m12
Colima, state	D4, n12
Colotlan	A1, 2
Comalcalco	D6
Comitán	C6
Compostela	m11
Concepción del Oro	C4, m13
Conchos, river	C3
Copala	D6
Cordoba	D5
Corozal	D7
Cortazar	C4, m13
Cosamaloapan	D5
Cotija de la Paz	B4
Cozumel	A3
Coyoacan	C4, m12
Cuauhtemoc	C4, k12
Cuajimalpa	m12
Cuautepec	m15
Cuautla	B4
Cuernavaca	D5, n14
Culhuacan	D5
Culiacan	C3
Cutzamala, river	n, o14
Distrito Federal (D.F.)	C4, m11
Dolores Hidalgo	m11
Durango, city	n14
Durango, state	n14
Ejutla de Crespo	B3
El Salto	C4
Eldorado	C3
Emiliano Zapata	D6
Encarnación de Díaz	m12
Ensenada	A1
Escuinapa	C3
Espita	C7
Exlava, river	h9
Fresnillo	C4
Frontera (Alvaro Obregon)	D6
Gertrude Sanchez	h9
Gómez Palacio	B3
Golfo de California	A2, 3; B2, 3
Gran Canal del Desagu	h9
Grande de Santiago, river	C2, 3
Grijalva, river	C3, 4; m11
Guadalajara	C4, m12
Guadalupe	A3
Guanajuato, city	C4, m13
Guanajuato, state	C4, m13
Guasave	B3
Guaymas	B2
Guerrero, state	D4, o13
Gulf of Mexico	C5, 6, 7, m15
Gustavo A. Madero	D5, 6
Gutiérrez Zamora	B2
Guzmán, Ciudad	m15
Hermosillo	A2
Hidalgo, Ciudad del	n13
Hidalgo, state	B3
Hidalgo del Parral	h9
Hondo, river	D5, o15
Huajuapan de Leon	C4
Huamantla	B3
Huatabampo	B2
Huatusco	D6
Huauchinango	n15
Huejotzingo	n14
Huetamo de Nuñez	h9
Huixtla	D6, E6
Huixtla	A2
Igualca	B2
Irapuato	C4
Isla Altamura, island	m13
Isla Angel de la Guarda, island	C3
Isla (I.) Cedros, island	A1
Isla Cerralvo, island	C4
Isla de Cozumel, island	D7
Isla Magdalena, island	B2
Isla San Jose, island	C2
Isla Santa Margarita, island	B2
Isla Tiburon, island	C3
Islas Tres Marias, islands	h9
Ixtacalco	n14
Ixtacihuatl, volcano	D5, o14
Ixtapalapa	D5, o14
Ixtepec, Ciudad	B2
Ixtlan del Rio	n14
Izamal	C7
Izucar de Matamoros	B4, C4
Jalapa Enriquez	C7
Jalisco, city	D6
Jalisco, state	C4, m12
Jalpan	C5, m14
Jerez de Garcia Salinas	C4
Jiménez, Ciudad	n14
Jojutla	C4
Juan Aldama	D6
Juarez	C6
Juarez, Ciudad	m11
Juchipila, river	C4
Juchitan	B3, 4
Lago (L.) de Chapala, lake	D6
Lago (L.) de Cuitzeo, lake	D7
Lago (L.) de Don Martin, lake	C4, m13
Lago (Lag.) de Magdalena, lake	D5
Lago (L.) de Patzcuaro, lake	C7
Lago (Lag.) de Sayula, lake	n14
Lago (L.) de Texcoco, dry lake	B3
Lagos de Moreno	m12
Laguna de Tamiahua, lagoon	g9
Laguna de Terminos, lagoon	n14
La Joya Madre, lagoon	D5, n14
La Paz	C2
La Piedad	m13
La Union	D5, n14
Leon	m13
Lerdo	C4
Lerma, river	D4, o13
Linares	C4, m13
Los Mochis	B4
Los Reyes	m13
Los Reyes Acozac	C5
Lower California, peninsula	B3
Madera, Ciudad	C5
Madero, Ciudad	C4
Magdalena	D6
Magdalena Contreras	h9
Manzanillo	C5
Mante, Ciudad	D4, n11
Matamoros (Coahuila)	B4
Matamoros (Tamaulipas)	B5
Mascala	C4
Mazatlán	C3
Mendoza, Ciudad	n15
Mexicali	C7
Mexico, state	A1
Mexico City	D5, n14; h9, 10
Michoacan state	D5, n14, h9
Miguel Auza	D4
Minatitlan	D6
Mineral del Monte	m14
Misantla	n14
Misteco, river	n14
Moctezuma, river	h9
Molino de Rosas	h9
Monclova	B4
Monterrey	B5
Morelia	D4, m13
Morelos, city	D5, n14
Morelos, state	n13
Moroleon	C7
Motul	D7
Muna	C7
Nativitas	D6
Naucalpan de Juarez, Ciudad de	h9
Navojoa	B3
Nayarit, state	B4
Nazas, river	C4
Nevado de Colima, mountain	n11
Nevado de Toluca, mountain	A2, n15
Nogales	B4
Nueva Rosita	B4
Nuevo Laredo	B4, 5, C4, 5
Nuevo Leon, state	D5, o15
Oaxaca, city	C4, m12
Oaxaca, state	B4
Obregón, Ciudad	n15
Ocotlan	n13
Ojinaga	C7
Orizaba	n15
Pachuca	C5, k14
Pacific Ocean	C, D, E 1, 2, 3, 4, 5, 6
Panuco	n14
Papantla	n11
Pariculin, volcano	n12
Parras de la Fuente	B4
Patzcuaro	n13
Penjamo	C7
Peto	n15
Pico de Orizaba, volcano	n15
Piedad, river	h9
Piedras Negras	B4
Popocatepetl, volcano	n15
Pozo Rica de Hidalgo	m15
Presa del Infiernillo, lake	D4, n12, 13
Presa Miguel Aleman, lake	D5, n15
Puebla, city	D5, n14, 15
Puebla, state	C3, m11
Puerto Vallarta	
Punta (Pta.) Abreojos, point	B2
Punta (Pta.) Arena, point	C3
Punta (Pta.) Concepcion, point	B2
Punta (Pta.) Mita, point	B1
Punta (Pta.) Eugenia, point	C3, m11
Punta (Pta.) Farallon, point	n11
Punta (Pta.) Ixtapa, point	D4, o13
Punta (Pta.) Morro, point	
Punta (Pta.) Rosa, point	B3
Punta (Pta.) San Felipe, point	A2
Punta San Juan de Lima, point	
Punta San Pablo, point	D4, n12
Puruandiro	B2
Queretaro, city	m13
Queretaro (QRO.), state	C4, m13
Quintana Roo, state	C4, 5, m13, 14
Remedios, river	D7
Reynosa	B5
Rincon de Romos	k12
Rio Balsas, river	D5, n14
Rio Colorado, river	C4
Rio Grande, city	A3, 4; B3, 4
Rio Grande, river	h9
Rioverde	m13
Rosario	C3
Sabinas Hidalgo	B4
Sahuayo	m12
Salamanca	B4, 5
Salina Cruz	D5
Saltillo	B4
San Andres Tetepilco	C7
San Andres Tototlapec	h9
San Andres Tuxtla	m13
San Borja, river	D5
San Cristóbal las Casas	C4, 5, k13, 14
San Francisco del Oro	m13
San Francisco del Rincon	h9
San Gabriel Chilas (Chilac)	C3, 4; m11
San Gregorio Atlapulco	A2
San Jeronimo Lidice	h9
San Juan de Aragon	h9
San Lorenzo Tezonco	h9
San Luis	A2
San Luis, river	B5
San Luis de la Paz	D4, m13
San Luis Potosi, city	D5
San Luis Potosi, state	D5, n14
San Miguel de Allende	m13
San Nicolas Tototlapan	h9
San Pedro, river	C7
San Pedro de las Colonias	D7
Santa Ana	h9
Santa Anita	A2
Santa Barbara	B3
Santa Fe	h9
Santa (Sta.) Maria, river	m14
Santa Rosalia	B2
Santa Ursula Coapa	h9
Santiago Papasquiaro	C3
Santiago Tepalcatlapan	h9
Santo Domingo, river	n15
Saucillo	B3
Sayula	D5, o15
Sector Popular	h9
Serdan, Ciudad	D4, n12
Sierra Madre, mountains	D6
Sierra de la Giganta, mountains	
Sierra Madre del Sur, mountains	B2, C2
Sierra Madre Occidental, mountains	
Sierra Madre Oriental, mountains	D4, 5, o13
Sierra Mojada, mountains	A, B, C, 3, 4
Sierra San Pedro Martir, mountains	B4, 5, C4, 5, m14
Sinaloa, town	A1
Sinaloa, state	m13
Sombrerete	B3
Sonora, state	A2, 3; B2, 3
Tabasco, state	D6
Tacambaro de Codallos	n13
Tamaulipas, state	B5, C5
Tampico	C5, k15
Tampico (Pto Alarcon)	n14
Tapachula	E6
Teapa	D6
Tecolutla, river	m15
Tecoman	D4, n12
Tecpan de Galeana	C3
Tecuala	D4
Tehuacan	D5, n15
Tehuantepec	D5
Tekax de Alvaro Obregon	C7
Teloloapan	D5, n14
Tenancingo	D5, n14
Tenosique	C7
Teocaltiche	C4, D6
Teocuitatlan	n12
Tepalcatepec	n12
Tepalcatepec, river	n12
Tepatitlan	n12
Tepeji del Rio	h9
Tepepan	C4, m11
Tepic	n14
Tequila	m12
Texcoco	n14
Teziutlan	g9
Ticoman	C7
Ticul	D5, n5
Tierra Blanca	A1
Tijuana	D7
Tikal, ruins (Guatemala)	h9
Tizapan	C7
Tizimin	h9
Tiacolula	C7
Tiacotalpan	D5
Tiahuac	D5
Tialnepantla	h9, n14
Tialnepantla, river	g9
Tlalpan	g9
Tlaltenco	o12
Tlapaneco, river	m12
Tlaquepaque	D5, n14
Tlaxcala, city	D5, n14
Tlaxcala, state	n14
Tlaxiaco	D5
Toluca	D6
Tonala	n15
Tonto, river	B4
Torreón	C5
Tula	C5, m4
Tulancingo	C3, m11
Tulyehualco	
Tuxpan (Nayarit)	B4
Tuxpan (Jalisco)	h9
Tuxpan, river	n15
Tuxpan de Rodriguez Cano (Veracruz)	C5, m15
Tuxtepec	n15
Tuxtla Gutierrez	D6
Union de Tula	n11
Uruapan	D4, n13
Usumacinta, river	D6
Uxmal, ruins	C7
Valladolid	C7
Valle de Santiago	m13
Valles, Ciudad de	B2
Venustiano Carranza	h9
Veracruz, city	C3
Veracruz, state	C, D5, m 15
Verde Grande Y de Belema, river	m12
Victoria Ciudad	C5
Villa de Mendez	B5
Villa Frontera	B4
Villa Obregon	h9
Villahermosa	D6
Xochimilco	h9, n14
Yaqui, river	A3, B3
Yautepec	n14
Yucatan, state	C7
Yucatan Channel	C7
Zacapu	n13
Zacatecas (ZAC.), state	C4, k13, m12
Zacoalco	C4, m12
Zamora de Hidalgo	C4, m12
Zapopan	m12
Zapotiltan	B4, m13
Zaragoza	
Zitacuaro	n14
Zumpango	n14

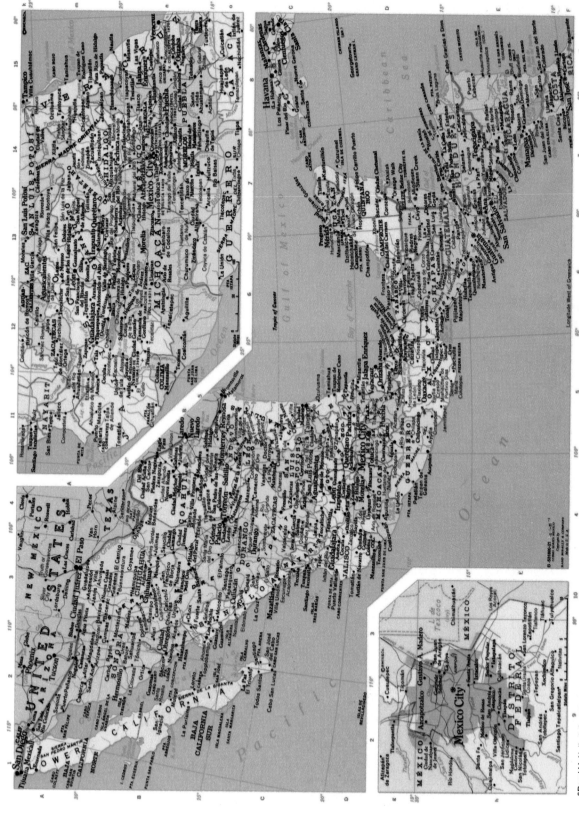

©Rand McNally & Co. R.L. 83-S-141

MINI-FACTS AT A GLANCE

GENERAL INFORMATION

Official Name: United Mexican States (*Estados Unidos Mexicanos*)

Capital: Mexico City

Language: Spanish

Government: Mexico is a federal republic with three branches of government—executive, legislative, and judicial. The president is very powerful. Unlike the president of the United States, the president of Mexico does not need approval of Congress to make important decisions. For example, in 1982, President José López Portillo nationalized Mexican banks. In 1976, President Luis Echeverría Álvarez devalued the Mexican peso. The president can appoint members of the cabinet, the attorney general, and diplomats, among other officials. He is entitled to only one six-year term of office. There is no vice-president. If the president dies, or otherwise cannot govern, the Senate elects a replacement until elections can be held. The legislative branch is composed of a Senate and a Chamber of Deputies. There are 128 senators who govern for six-year terms. The Chamber of Deputies has five hundred members, who serve three-year terms. There are thirty-two "states" in Mexico, including two territories and a federal district much like the District of Columbia in the United States. Among the states that are not a territory or the federal district, each has its own popularly elected governor and constitution. The two territories have governors appointed by the president. The federal district is governed by a *jefe* (chief) or *regente* (regent) also appointed by the president. State governors who are elected serve six-year terms. Mexico is basically a one-party country. Although there are others, the official party is the *Partido Revolucionario Institucional* (Institutional Revolutionary party).

Flag: The national flag has three vertical bands. From left to right they are green, white, and red. In the center of the white band is the country's coat of arms. Of the three colors on the flag, green stands for independence, white for religion, and red for union. The flag was adopted in 1821.

Coat of Arms: The coat of arms is an eagle with a snake in its beak.

National Song: *"Mexicanos, al grito de guerra"* ("Mexicans, at the war cry")

Religion: Over 90 percent of all Mexicans are Roman Catholic. Most of the rest are Protestant or Jewish.

Money: Money in Mexico is measured in pesos. One peso is divided into 100 centavos. In January 1996 the exchange rate between Mexican pesos and American dollars was 7.56 pesos to 1 dollar.

Weights and Measures: Mexico uses the metric system.

Membership in International Organizations: Latin American Economic System (SELA); Latin American Integration Association (LAIA); Organization of American States (OAS); United Nations (UN)

Population: 95,939,000 (mid-1994 estimate). Distribution is 71 percent urban, 29 percent rural. Density is 127 persons per square mile (49 persons per km²)

Cities:	1990 Census
Mexico City	10,000,000
Guadalajara	1,650,205
Netzahualcóyotl	1,255,456
Monterrey	1,069,238
Puebla	1,007,170
Cuidad Juárez	798,499
León	758,279

GEOGRAPHY

Highest Point: Orizaba (Citlaltéptl Volcano), 18,701 ft. (5,700 m)

Lowest Point: Near Mexicali, 33 ft. (10 m) below sea level

Coastline: 6,320 mi. (10,170 km)

Mountains: Most of Mexico is composed of mountains and plateaus. Except for the Yucatán Peninsula and the eastern and northwestern coastal plains (only 14 percent of the country), the average altitude is more than 3,300 ft. (1,005.8 m), but nearly 71 percent of the country lies at about 1,600 ft. (487.68 m) above sea level. Some mountain ranges are volcanic, including the *Sierra Volcanica Transversal* (Transversal Volcanic Mountain Range) and the *Neo-Volcanica Cordillera* (New Volcanic Range).

Climate: In Mexico, mountains, not latitudes, determine the climate. Most of Mexico is very dry. Only about 12 percent of the total area gets enough rainfall in all seasons. Half of Mexico receives less than 24 in. (60.96 cm) of precipitation annually. Although the coastal areas get the benefit of humid trade winds and tropical hurricanes, which occur in the late summer and early fall, the precipitation falls mostly in the mountains near the coast, leaving the interior very dry. The least amount of rainfall—2 to 4 in. (5.08 to 10.16 cm)—falls in the Baja California peninsula. The most—100 to 180 in. (254 to 457 cm)—falls in the Sierra Madre Oriental in north Oaxaca and Chiapas, in the Tuxtlas Massif, and the Sierra de Soconusco near the border with Guatemala in the southwest.

Temperatures in Mexico go from tropical in the coastal lowlands to cool in the higher mountains. In Manzanillo, a port on the hot, tropical Pacific coast, the mean temperature is approximately 79° F. (26° C), although it fluctuates between 73° and 84° F. (23° and 29° C). Tepic, at 3,000 ft. (914.4 m) above sea level, has an average temperature of 68° F. (20° C), although it varies between 57° and 82° F. (14° and 28° C). In the north, in Chihuahua, at 4,700 ft. (1,432.5 m), there is a great difference between June and January mean temperatures—79° F. (26° C) and 50° F. (10° C), respectively. In some regions, such as the plateaus, the dry northwest, and the high Sierra Madres, the temperature sometimes drops below freezing.

Greatest Distances: North to south — 1,250 mi. (2,012 km)
East to west — 1,900 mi. (3,060 km)

Area: 758,136 sq. mi. (1,963,564 km²), including 2,071 sq. mi. (5,364 km²) of outlying islands

NATURE

Vegetation: In the northern, northwest, and central regions — cactus, agave, cassava, mesquite or scrub, and brush plants. In the south and east, in Yucatán, and on the western coasts — rain forests, savanna (grassland), and spiny plants. In the central mountains and the Sierra Madres — at altitudes of 5,000 to 13,000 ft. (1,524 to 3,962 m) — evergreens, German oak, and other varieties of deciduous trees. On the coasts: large mangrove swamps.

Fish, coastal: Tuna, marlin, swordfish, tarpon, sardines, abalone, shrimp, oysters

Fish, inland: Trout

Animals: Bears, deer, mountain lions, jaguars, coyotes, monkeys, alligators, rodents, armadillos, tapirs, anteaters, wolves

Birds: Quetzals, herons, parrots, pelicans, hummingbirds, flamingos

EVERYDAY LIFE

Food: The tortilla forms the basis of most Mexican dishes. It is a round, thin cake of unleavened cornmeal. Enchiladas and tacos are folded or rolled tortillas filled with meat, chicken, or cheese. Enchiladas are usually covered with a sauce. Nearly every Mexican meal is served with beans. Often they are mashed and served as *frijoles refritos* (refried beans). Rice, too, accompanies most meals. Contrary to popular belief, all Mexican food is not spicy hot. But whether eaten in a restaurant or in a private home, meals are served with side dishes of hot chili sauce or whole chili peppers. Mexican desserts include flan (a custard pudding), and some popular drinks are hot chocolate and a variety of fruit drinks called *liquados.*

Housing: Though wealthy Mexicans live in modern apartment buildings and houses in the cities and suburbs, there is not enough decent housing at affordable prices for most Mexicans. Many city housing units are substandard and have poor water supplies. Most of the unemployed who come to the cities to find work are forced to live in the growing slum areas. In the country, where many Mexicans live on *ejidos*, or collective farms, small homes are built of adobe brick. Most farmhouses have one or two rooms in which children, parents, and grandparents live together. Family members sleep on straw mats called *petates*, spread over a hard-packed dirt floor. Remote areas have no electricity or reliable sources of drinking water. Many of the poorest houses, however, are brightened by well-tended gardens or pots of flowers. In Yucatán, Indians build round or rectangular houses with roofs of palm leaves.

Holidays:

January 1 (New Year's Day)
February 5 (Constitution Day)
March 21 (Birthday of Benito Juárez)
Easter
May 1 (Labor Day)
May 5, *Cinco de Mayo* (Anniversary of the Battle of Puebla)
September 1 (President's Annual Message)
September 16 (Independence Day)
October 12, *Dia de la Raza* (Columbus Day; Day of the Race)
November 2, *Dia de los Muertos* (All Souls' Day; Day of the Dead)
November 20 (Anniversary of the Revolution)
December 12 (Day of Our Lady of Guadalupe)
December 24-25 (Christmas)

Culture: In recent years, the cultural life of Mexico has had more to do with national than regional affairs. For example, Mexican literature no longer deals with revolution alone. Although the sufferings of the Mexican peasant are still considered important, modern writers tend to write about other things. Important writers in current Mexican literature include Juan José Arreola, Carlos Fuentes, and Octavio Paz. Mexico has eight major symphony orchestras and five choruses. But rock music is also popular. *Mariachi* bands, whose original purpose was to serenade Mexican maidens during courtship, and groups of *nortenos,* or singing cowboys whose music can be compared to American country and western music, play music that is native to Mexico. Many Mexican movies deal with historical subjects, though *Los Olvidados,* an important 1950 film, told the story of an adolescent farm boy lost on the streets of Mexico City. Mexican artists are world famous for their mural painting. Even in Maya and Aztec times, murals were in evidence. In modern times, Mexican muralists reached their height during the 1910-20 Revolution. Three outstanding muralists who worked during that era were José Orozco, Diego Rivera, and David Siqueiros. Because Mexican society was in such turmoil during the Revolution, many of their murals were political in subject matter. Mexican folk art is renowned throughout the world. Mexican silversmiths and jewelers fashion exquisite pieces. Entire mountain villages are known for their production of certain handicrafts, including blue tiles, straw baskets, blown-glass figurines, and pottery.

Sports and Recreation: The most popular sport in Mexico is soccer, with baseball a close second. The Mexican baseball league attracts almost as many fans as does the soccer league. Mexicans excel in many other sports as well. Their tennis players are strong in world competition and their race walkers have long dominated the Olympics. The Spaniards brought bullfighting to Mexico and it remains a popular attraction. Also popular are the Mexican rodeos called *charriadas.* American rodeo performers marvel at the skills displayed by Mexican horsemen called *charros.*

Communications: Mexico has about 300 newspapers, with about 20 Mexico City papers accounting for nearly 50 percent of the total 11.4 million circulation. There are about 1,524 radio stations and about 537 television stations. The country is served by an extensive network of telephone and telegraph lines.

Transportation: Mexico's land transportation system is one of the most advanced in Latin America. There are nearly 18,642 mi. (30,000 km) of railroads, which are government owned. In 1992, there were 150,355 mi. (241,962 km) of roads, including three sections of the Pan American Highway. The rugged mountains and thick jungles of Mexico encourage air travel, and there are twenty-eight international and twenty national airports. Aerovías de México (AeroMexico) is the national airline. In recent years, the Mexican government has been investing millions of pesos in industrial ports such as those at Tampico, Coatzacoalcos, and Salina Cruz.

Education: In Mexico, primary education is free. All children must attend seven years of primary school and three years of secondary education. The illiteracy rate among Mexicans, which was 29 percent in 1960, dropped to 12.7 percent in 1990. In 1993-94, there were some 300 institutions of higher learning, including more than 80 universities. There are hundreds of vocational and professional schools.

Health: Because of attempts by the government to provide better health care, the health of Mexicans has improved greatly in recent years. However, there are still many cases of infectious diseases that affect the intestines, and bad diets still cause diseases such as rickets, anemia, and vitamin deficiency. There are also many cases of tonsilitis, flu, and respiratory disease.

IMPORTANT DATES

about 40,000 B.C.—Human beings arrive in northern Mexico

3114 B.C.—Beginning of the Maya calendar

about 3000 B.C.—Ancient Mexicans discover how to grow maize (corn)

about 1200 to 100 B.C.—Olmec live in what is the present-day state of Veracruz

A.D. 100—Rise of the city of Teotihuacán

200-800—Maya civilization reaches its zenith

850—Maya builders stop building great cities

300-900—Classical Period (Golden Age) of Mesoamerican history

900s—Toltec rule in the Valley of Mexico

1400s—Aztec reach height of their power

1502—Montezuma becomes emperor of the Aztec

1519—Hernando Cortés lands in Mexico

1520—Aztec drive foreigners out of the city of Tenochtítlan

1521—Cortés takes Tenochtítlan

1521-1821—Spain rules Mexico

1531—Indian Juan Diego sees the Virgin of Guadalupe

1810—Revolution, led by Miguel Hidalgo y Castilla, begins

1811—Hidalgo executed

1813—At the instigation of José Maria Morelos y Pavón, the Congress of Chilpancingo issues a declaration of independence from Spain

1815—Morelos executed

1821—Mexico declared an independent nation

1824—First Mexican constitution adopted; federal republic declared

1836—New constitution drawn up; Texas declares itself an independent nation; Mexican General Antonio López de Santa Anna and his troops win Battle of the Alamo in San Antonio, Texas

1846—War between Mexico and the United States

1848—Treaty of Guadalupe Hidalgo ends war between Mexico and United States; Mexico cedes to United States 918,355 sq. mi. (2,378,530 km²) of territory including present states of Texas, California, New Mexico, Nevada, Utah, Arizona, and part of Colorado

1858—Benito Juárez becomes president during a civil war

1862—Napoleon III invades Mexico and is defeated by Mexican forces

1863—Napoleon III sends in larger army; Juárez flees to United States

1864-67—Maximilian, named emperor of Mexico by Napoleon III, rules Mexico

1867—Maximilian executed by Juárez

1872—Juárez dies of heart attack

1877—Porfirio Díaz becomes president; except for brief period, rules until 1911

1910—Liberal landowner Francisco Madero calls for revolution

1911—Madero elected first revolutionary president

1913—Counterrevolutionary dictator Victoriano Huerta seizes power and executes Madero; full-scale revolution begins

1913-20—Ten different presidents rule Mexico

1914—United States Marines land at Veracruz to help main revolutionary movement

1917—New constitution reflects social and political goals of the revolution

1920—Álvaro Obregón becomes president; restores peace

1929—President Elías Calles creates National Revolutionary party (now PRI)

1938—President Lázaro Cárdenas nationalizes petroleum industry

1942—Mexico declares war on Axis powers

1946—Election of President Miguel Alemán Valdés begins unbroken line of civilian presidents

1952—Election of President Adolpho Ruiz Cortines

1958—Election of President Adolfo López Mateos

1964—Election of President Gustavo Díaz Ordaz

1970—Election of President Luis Echeverría Álvarez

1976—Echeverría devalues peso; election of President José López Portillo

1982—Country on verge of bankruptcy; Portillo nationalizes banks; election of President Miguel de la Madrid Hurtado

1985—Two disasterous earthquakes shake south central Mexico, killing more than 10,000

1988—Hurricane Gilbert destroys the homes of 30,000 residents of the Yucatán Peninsula; the presidential election brings an end to the one-party system in Mexico; the ruling Institutional Revolutionary Party loses its wide leads in the Senate and Chamber of Deputies; Carlos Salinas de Gortari becomes president and begins an entire reform program

1989—An earthquake, measuring 7.0 on the Richter scale, injures hundreds near Mexico City

1990—The government reports that the inflation rate of 30% is the lowest since 1978; banks agree to debt-reduction pact in hopes of spurring economic growth and investments; many companies run by the government become private companies that can now provide work with the most modern equipment

1991—The inflation rate of 18.8% continues to be reduced, and the growth rate continues to rise

1992—Mexico joins the Debt for Nature swap, by which countries can have part of their foreign loan debt reduced if 40 percent of the forgiven amount is spent on environmental restoration; nearly half the children born in one of Mexico City's major hospitals have enough lead in their blood to cause permanent physical and mental problems, according to medical reports; full diplomatic relations are established with the Vatican

1993—The United States sets tariffs on imported Mexican steel meant to reduce the amount of steel being imported from Mexico and increase U.S. steel production; new peso currency is introduced equivalent to 1,000 former pesos

1994—The North American Free Trade Agreement (NAFTA) between Mexico, Canada, and the United States takes effect; uprisings by the rebel Zapatista National Liberation Army (EZLN) result in government promises to improve living standards of the indigenous Indians; with UN officials monitoring presidential elections, Ernesto Zedillo Ponce de León of the PRI is elected president

1995—Hurricane Roxanne and Hurricane Opal hit the Gulf of Mexico; an earthquake kills about 60 people in Manzanillo on the Pacific Coast; Raúl Salinas de Gortari, brother of former president Carlos Salinas de Gortari, is arrested on charges of corruption and involvement in political assassination; the old peso currency is withdrawn from the market; the government is accused by human rights groups of trying to cover up many violations

1996—A $3.5 million military helicopter base is being built in Oaxaca City, in one of the poorest states in Mexico with a large Indian population

*Mexicans
take great pride
in their
flower gardens.*

IMPORTANT PEOPLE

Miguel Alemán Valdés (1902-   ), president of Mexico, 1946-52

Ignacio Allende (1779-1811), one of the leaders of the 1810 revolution

Ignacio Manuel Altamirano (1834-93), poet

Bobby Avila, Cleveland Indians baseball star in the 1950s

Plutarco Elías Calles (1877-1945), Mexican general; president of Mexico, 1924-28

Lázaro Cárdenas (1895-1970), president of Mexico, 1934-40; nationalized oil
    industry

Carlota (1840-1927), empress of Mexico, 1864-67

Venustiano Carranza (1859-1920), president of Mexico, 1915-20

Hernando Cortés (1485-1547), Spanish conqueror of Mexico

Juana Inés de la Cruz (1648?-1695), author, poet, playwright

Porfirio Díaz (1830-1915), president of Mexico, 1877-80 and 1884-1911

Juan Diego, Indian who saw Virgin of Guadalupe in 1531

Luis Echeverría Álvarez (1922-   ), president of Mexico, 1970-76

José Joaquín Fernández de Lizardi (1776-1827), political author and leading literary figure during the struggle for independence; the first novelist in Spanish America

Manuel González (1833-93), Mexican general; president of Mexico, 1880-84

Vincente Guerrero (1783-1831), Mexican leader during first revolutionary period; president of Mexico in 1829

Martín Luis Guzmán (1887-1976), novelist, essayist, newspaperman, politician

Miguel Hidalgo y Castilla (1753-1811), began the first Mexican revolution on September 16, 1810; executed by Spanish authorities on July 30, 1811

Victoriano Huerta (1854-1916), provisional president of Mexico, 1913-14

Agustín de Iturbide (1783-1824), emperor of Mexico, 1822-23

Benito Juárez (1806-72), president of Mexico, 1857-72

Adolfo López Mateos (1910-69), president of Mexico, 1958-64

Jose López Portillo, president of Mexico, 1976-82

Francisco Madero (1873-1913), president of Mexico, 1911-13

Miguel de la Madrid Hurtado (1935-   ), president of Mexico, 1982-88

Maximilian (1832-67), emperor of Mexico, 1864-67

Montezuma II (1466-1520), last Aztec emperor of Mexico, 1502-20

José María Morelos y Pavón (1765-1815), revolutionary leader under whose instigation Chilpancingo Congress issued declaration of independence from Spain

Napoleon III (1808-73), emperor of France and conqueror of Mexico

Álvaro Obregón (1880-1928), president of Mexico, 1920-24

Gustavo Díaz Ordaz (1911-   ), president of Mexico, 1964-70

José Orozco (1883-1949), muralist

Octavio Paz (1914-), author

Alfonso Reyes (1889-1959), diplomat, author, playwright, essayist

Diego Rivera (1886-1957), muralist

Alfonso García Robles (1911-   ), diplomat, shared 1982 Nobel Peace Prize for his work on behalf of disarmament

Ignacio Rodríguez Galván (1816-42), poet

Adolpho Ruiz Cortines (1891-1973), president of Mexico, 1952-58

Juan Rulfo (1918-86), novelist

David Alfaro Siqueiros (1898-1974), muralist

Guadalupe Victoria (1789-1843), first president of the republic, 1824-29

Pancho Villa (1877-1923), revolutionary leader

Emiliano Zapata (1879-1919), revolutionary leader

Brightly painted buildings in a small Mexican town

INDEX

Page numbers that appear in boldface type indicate illustrations.

About the Author

　R. Conrad Stein was born and grew up in Chicago. He attended the University of Illinois, where he earned a degree in history. He is the author of dozens of other books for young readers. Mr. Stein is married to Deborah Kent, a writer of books for teenage readers.

　Mexico is Mr. Stein's second home. He lived in the country for seven years. He speaks Spanish and holds an advanced degree from the University of Guanajuato. He was delighted when Childrens Press asked him to write this book about Mexico, his adopted country.